PIZZA

James McNair

Photography by Patricia Brabant
Chronicle Books • San Francisco

Printed in Japan by Toppan Printing Co.,
Tokyo

Library of Congress Cataloging-in-
Publication Data
McNair, James K.
Pizza / James McNair ;
photography by Patricia Brabant.
p. cm.
Includes index.
ISBN 0-87701-481-7.
ISBN 0-87701-448-5 (pbk.)
1. Pizza   I. Title
TX770.P58M36 1987
641.8'24—dc19
87-17381 CIP

Distributed in Canada by
Raincoast Books
112 East Third Avenue
Vancouver, British Columbia
V5T 1C8
10 9 8 7 6

Chronicle Books
San Francisco, California

To Marian May (aka Mimma Foggi), a true Italian, editor extraordinaire, and devoted friend, who has encouraged my writing career through the years and helped me to believe in my abilities even during the lean times.

And in memory of Chuck Thayer, a congenial man and diligent professional, who, with his associates, produced the type and mechanicals for my last three books.

Produced by The Rockpile Press, San Francisco and Lake Tahoe

Art direction, photographic and food styling, and book design
by James McNair

Editorial production assistance by Lin Cotton

Studio kitchen assistance by Gail High

Photography assistance by Sheryl Scott

Typography and mechanical production by Cleve Gallat and Peter Linato
of Chuck Thayer Associates, Ltd.

CONTENTS

OUR NUMBER-ONE FOOD

Contrary to the popular belief that it is very fattening, pizza, minus sausage and other highly caloric toppings, has a nutrition profile that shows it to be a near-perfect food. In fact, it supplies basic nutrients in almost the exact amounts recommended in the Dietary Goals for the United States outlined by the Senate Select Committee on Nutrition and Human Needs: 15 percent protein, 27 percent fat, and 58 percent carbohydrate. With this good news in mind, coupled with your about-to-be-acquired skills in pizza making, enjoy this favorite food frequently.

Pizza has become more American than mom's apple pie. According to the latest statistics from the National Restaurant Association, pizzerias, confined mostly to Little Italies on this side of the Atlantic until the mid-1940s, now outnumber sellers of our native hamburger. Chains featuring this longtime favorite have set up shop across the country and around the globe. The largest, Pizza Hut, alone has 4,500 outlets that serve over 8 million pizza lovers each year.

Despite its nationwide popularity, don't let anyone tell you that pizza was created here. For years I'd heard the myth that, like Chinese chop suey, it was invented by immigrants to appeal to the American palate. I learned better a decade ago when I spent time in Italy doing research for a book on that country's unsurpassed cuisine.

Established in Naples in 1830, Port'Alba is reputed to be the world's first true pizzeria. Lava rock from nearby Mount Vesuvius was used to line the wood-fired oven of this innovator, a fact that I'm sure makes the owners of today's trendy pizzerias green with envy. The residents of the boot, however, are known to have been eating some form of pizza long before Port'Alba opened. Historical documents tell of the Romans enjoying rounds of seasoned oven-baked bread during the first century, an idea they most likely borrowed from the Greeks and Etruscans. By the year 1000, *picea,* a disk of dough generously dusted with herbs and spices, was common in Naples.

Pizza started out as a snack for Italian women who needed to satisfy hunger pangs while waiting for their bread to bake in the town's communal ovens. A *signora* would break off a piece of the dough, flatten it out, and top it with whatever seasonings were on hand, then quickly bake it.

These pizzas were, of course, baked without today's ubiquitous tomato crown. Two hundred years passed from the time the tomato was introduced to the Continent from Peru by one of Columbus's sailors until the Neapolitans were able to muster the courage to eat the strictly ornamental fruit that was thought to be poisonous. The course of pizza was altered forever once the Italians discovered the great taste of *pomidori,* or "golden fruit," named for the bright yellow color of the early varieties. Although it's hard to imagine, cheese was not added to pizza until 1889, when baker Raffaele Esposito of Pietro il Pizzaiolo pizzeria was issued a royal summons to prepare pizza for Queen Margherita. To salute the colors of the Italian flag, Esposito added a new ingredient, white mozzarella, to the traditional Naples pairing of red tomato and green basil.

Italian immigrant Gennaro Lombardi opened the first American pizzeria in New York City in 1905, where he served a variation of the Neapolitan pie. Pizza remained restricted to the Italian neighborhoods of American cities until the end of World War II, when great waves of soldiers returning from duty in Italy were intent upon introducing it to their friends and families. Demand soon pushed the pizzeria into new districts where it could cater to the general public, who quickly learned to love the pie.

During a recent National Pizza Week, the United States Department of Agriculture released these statistics:

- **Americans eat 11 billion slices of pizza each year.**

- **The annual per capita pizza consumption is 23 pounds.**

- **Thin-crust pizzas are preferred over thick-crust pizzas by 48 percent to 45 percent.**

- **The favorite pizza topping is pepperoni; the least favorite is anchovies.**

- **Saturday night is the biggest night of the week for eating pizza.**

- **More than $1 billion was spent on 450 million pounds of frozen pizza in a recent year, making pizza one of the fastest-selling prepared foods in America.**

- **In the United States, pizza represents an $11-billion-a-year industry.**

- **In Italian, *pizza* means "pie," so pizza pie is redundant.**

USING THIS BOOK

This book contains recipes for two styles of pizza—traditional and new. You'll discover directions for baking authentic Italian, French, New York, and Chicago pies, all of which are wonderful. But for me the most exciting section of the book is the collection of recipes that reflect the new gourmet status of what started out as a snack for Old World peasants.

The next few pages will take you, step-by-step, through the procedure for making perfect pizza. Please don't attempt the recipes until you've become fully familiar with the techniques involved.

My own discovery of the comforting pleasures of pizza took place in New York City, since the exotic pie had yet to make inroads into Louisiana when I left there to conquer Manhattan. Before then I'd only eaten pizza a few times: the version rendered by a not-very-good New Orleans pizzeria and my adolescent sister's interpretations of a mix from the grocer's shelves. My very first dinner in the Big Apple was at Al Buon Gusto, a Columbus Avenue pizzeria just around the corner from my West Seventy-second Street apartment. Through my years in New York I repeated that short trip countless times to enjoy pizza with my friends Carol Faulkner and C.C. and Ragan Courtney.

One day when my family was visiting from Louisiana, my daddy volunteered to go around the corner for take-out pizza. He was gone for what seemed like a very long time just to pick up a few slices, which in any case were always ready to go. When I finally opened the door following his ring, there he stood, grinning and blushing at his obvious mistake, holding a stack of five enormous pizza boxes. Not being very knowledgeable about the culture of the pizzeria, he'd ordered one large pie per person. Needless to say, we munched leftover pizza until we couldn't look at another piece.

I'll never forget a lucky chance encounter with pizza on my first trip to Italy. I was traveling with my friend Lenny Meyer and Venice was our initial stop. A sudden Venetian downpour forced us to duck under the canopy of a tiny pizzeria for protection. Since we were trapped there, we thought we might as well order the house specialty. It was my first pizza in the country of its origin. I thought I had arrived in heaven. And the pizza only got better during travels farther south.

MAKING PERFECT PIZZA

For far too long I suffered under the delusion that pizza making was a difficult task best left to the pros. Besides, how could I even begin to approach the results of a wood-fired brick oven at home? A few quarry tiles, a few pounds of flour, and a few hours in the kitchen quickly got me past my fears. Now home-baked pizza regularly appears on my table, with successes that include some of the best versions I've eaten on either side of the Atlantic.

All you need to get going are the proper ingredients; some special equipment; an understanding of the basic techniques of mixing, kneading, shaping, filling, and baking the dough; and a little practice.

Ingredients

OILS

The addition of olive oil to pizza dough creates a crisp crust with a tender interior. I also usually brush it on the dough before cooking to keep the crust from drying out during baking and to insure a golden brown color. Plus, I like to swab the edges of the crust with oil as soon as the pizza comes out of the oven to add a little moisture and flavor.

The nature of olive oil varies according to the method by which it was produced. Extra-virgin olive oil is the best quality and therefore the most expensive. The finest olives are pressed by hand to produce it. I prefer its rich green color and fresh flavor. Olive oil labeled simply "virgin" is made from the first pressing of olives of lesser quality; it is quite good, but less fruity tasting than extra-virgin. If you prefer a lighter-tasting olive oil, look for the golden color of "pure" olive oil, produced from the second or third pressing of the olives.

I use lightly flavored vegetable oil for greasing screens and pans and in recipes where olive oil would overwhelm or not be compatible with the toppings. You'll also encounter intensely flavored walnut oil, Asian-style sesame oil, and hot chili oil, all of which add unique character to nontraditional pizzas.

Pizza is a simple dish—a crisp and chewy bread topped with good foods full of natural flavors. For the best pizzas you'll ever eat, the rule is also simple: use only the freshest and finest ingredients available.

Flours. For well-textured, extra-crispy crusts, choose bread flour or semolina flour. Bread flour, used by most pizzerias, is made from hard northern spring wheat. It has a high gluten content that raises yeast dough to its maximum volume, which results in a dough that can be stretched quite thinly. Semolina flour, the same type used in quality dried pasta, is milled from hard durum wheat. It requires the addition of a little more water to the dough than is necessary with bread flour. Dough made of semolina or bread flour takes longer to knead and rise than dough made with all-purpose flour, but the very crispy crusts make the extra effort and time worthwhile.

Though unbleached all-purpose flour is a blend of hard and soft wheats, its gluten content is high enough to make excellent crusts. It requires less moisture, kneading, and rising time than bread or semolina flours. If you use unbleached all-purpose flour, omit the second rising described in the Basic Pizza Dough recipe.

The amount of flour you'll end up kneading into the dough depends on the type of flour used, as already explained, and the amount of moisture in the air. When humidity is high, the dough will be sticky and more flour will need to be added. If the dough is too dry, you must add extra water; be sure to add it only a small bit at a time to prevent the dough from becoming too wet.

Yeasts. Choose either active dry yeast or the relatively new quick-rising dry yeast, which cuts the rising time of dough by about 20 percent. Whichever form of granulated yeast you choose, always check its expiration date before using. Read more about yeast in the Basic Pizza Dough recipe on page 16.

Cheeses. Contrary to the popular belief that pizza is always a cheese-and-tomato pie, you can make great pizzas without any cheese. Smooth-melting cheeses are, however, essential to the success of many pizzas and mozzarella is the type used most often. Unfortunately, the majority of widely available factory-made mozzarella melts into a rubbery mass. Excellent alternatives include fresh mozzarella that's made daily by hand in large Italian communities throughout the United States, or mozzarella imported from Italy, especially the variety made in part from water buffalo's milk. If you locate these fresh cheeses but can't use them that day, store them up to a couple of days immersed in a solution of water mixed with a little skimmed milk; change the solution daily.

If you don't have access to fresh mozzarella, here are a few tips to prevent commercial cheese from becoming rubbery. Shred or chop the cheese instead of slicing it; it will melt more smoothly. Marcella Hazan, doyenne of Italian cooking, advocates soaking shredded factory-made mozzarella in olive oil for about an hour before cooking to approximate the creaminess of its Italian counterpart. Blending mozzarella with other good-melting cheeses also results in a creamy melt. Carrie Crotty, owner of the famed Antiguan pizzeria Pizzas in Paradise, tells me that she uses two parts mozzarella to one part English white Cheddar. I mix mozzarella with Italian Fontina or Provolone, Holland Gouda, French Gruyère, Vermont Cheddar, California Monterey Jack, or any other cheese that melts nicely. Often I forget the mozzarella and use these and other cheeses in combination or alone. Be adventuresome and try your favorites; chances are they'll work.

I often finish off a fresh-from-the-oven pizza with Parmesan cheese. If you don't go with top-of-the-line Parmigiano Reggiano, which is costly but definitely worth it, choose the best similar grating cheese you can find. Italy protects the real thing with restricted labeling; similar Italian cheeses must be tagged grana. Some cheeses produced outside of Italy are labeled Parmesan, but bear little resemblance to the classic. Others, such as Asiago or a few domestic "Parmesans," are decent substitutes. Just don't even think of using that stuff out of a green box on one of my pizzas!

TOMATOES

Vine-ripened tomatoes, preferably the Italian plum varieties, or canned plum tomatoes are the preferred choices. Most fresh tomatoes sold in supermarkets have been developed for shipping and long storage, resulting in tasteless fruit. When you can't find plum tomatoes, keep in mind that cherry tomatoes usually have pretty good flavor. Tomatoes, you may be surprised to discover, are not called for in the majority of recipes in this book. As with cheese, they are not *de rigueur* for first-rate pizza.

SAUCES

Please forget about canned pizza sauces. When a recipe calls for tomato sauce—although most of mine don't—make your own simple version from flavorful ripe or canned tomatoes. In this book you'll discover some surprising sauces, from Chinese *hoisin* to Southern-style barbecue, that add new dimensions to pizza.

When sauce is added to a pizza, reverse the common pizzeria order of ingredients. Put a layer of cheese over the dough before adding sauce; the cheese seals the crust and prevents it from getting soggy which is often the case when the sauce is in direct contact with the dough.

Equipment

EASY MIXING

I strongly recommend a *heavy-duty standing electric mixer* with a dough hook for quick and easy mixing and kneading pizza dough.

A *dough scraper* is essential if you knead dough by hand. This wood-handled utensil has a flexible metal blade for prying up sticky dough from work surfaces.

In addition to mixing bowls, a rolling pin, and other basic equipment you most likely have on hand, here is a list of special tools for successful pizza making. Some are essential; others are merely desirable. Most can be found at kitchen shops or restaurant-supply stores.

Unglazed quarry tile. Made of hard clay similar to that used in pizza ovens in Italy, quarry tiles provide the dry, intense direct heat that is necessary to achieve crisp crusts in a home oven. Measure the floor of your oven, allowing for a tile-free 1-inch border for air circulation. Take the measurement with you to a ceramic tile supplier and purchase unglazed tiles that will fill this area, having some cut to fit as needed. Look for tiles that are slightly less than ½ inch thick; tiles that are thicker than that take too long to heat up, while thinner ones may crack from the intense heat.

To use the tiles in a gas oven, remove the oven racks and line the oven floor with the tiles. In an electric oven, place the oven rack on the lowest position and line it with the tiles. In either case, preheat the oven to 500° F. for 1 hour before baking.

Baking stone. Several types of baking stone are marketed that work on the same principal as quarry tiles. Averaging about 14 inches in diameter, they limit the size of the pizza and are costlier than tiles, but they are also less bulky to store and easier to install in the oven. If you decide to purchase a baking stone, keep in mind that a rectangular shape allows greater flexibility in pizza size and shape. When cooking a small pizza for myself, however, I find a round stone the best choice.

Pizza peel. This long-handled instrument with a flat paddle-shaped foot is used by professional pizza bakers to transport the pizza to and from the hot baking surface. Wooden peels are best, though more expensive than metal ones. Both range in size from around 10 inches to 2 feet in diameter. Select a peel that will easily fit inside your oven and has a broad end only slightly larger than the size pizzas you plan to make. Measure to be sure that the overall length—from handle tip to end of paddle—is not so long that you can't turn freely in the space between your oven and the nearest obstacle. It takes practice to master the correct jerky movements for maneuvering the pizza around on the peel, so don't be too discouraged if a couple of pies end up in a heap on the tiles or the kitchen floor. The superb crusts are worth the trouble of learning to use the peel.

Pizza screen. If you're leery of using the pizza peel to transport the pizza to and from the stone baking surface, or if you enjoy large pizzas or ones with weighty toppings, I highly recommend a flat round of heavy wire mesh bordered with strong wire tape as a surefire way of retrieving the pie without danger of spilling it. The pizza screen also allows you to transport several small pizzas or calzone to the oven at once, which comes in handy when making appetizers. Pizza screens are available from 8 inches to 2 feet in diameter. Choose one that will fit comfortably within your oven. Brush or spray the screen with vegetable oil before assembling the pizza directly on it, then place it on the preheated tiles. If you decide to bake on the screen without the tiles, set it on an oven rack inserted in the middle or top position.

Pans. Deep-dish pans made of heavy-gauge black steel are recommended for baking deep-dish pizzas. They retain more heat than those of shiny aluminum, resulting in a crispier crust. Round pans vary from 6 to 18 inches in diameter; square pans usually measure 12 or 14 inches. Select one that is 1½ to 2 inches deep and heavy enough to withstand intense heat without warping. Try to find pans with removable bottoms, like quiche or tart pans, for easier freeing of the pizza.

Before using a black-steel pan for the first time, season it by washing in sudsy hot water, rinsing, and drying thoroughly. Then pour about 1 tablespoon vegetable oil on a paper towel and evenly rub it over the pan bottom and sides. Place the pan in a 325° F. oven and heat for 45 minutes. Remove from the oven, cool, and then wipe away any excess oil with paper towels. Avoid scouring the pan, or the well-seasoned surface will be lost and crusts will stick. Never cut the pizza while it is still in the pan; the dough will cling to the cut marks in the future. Rub the pan with vegetable oil each time before using.

I do not recommend the use of tray pans for baking thin-crusted flat pizzas, with the exception of a new type that is perforated on the bottom to simulate a pizza screen and allow direct heat to reach the crust. If you prefer thick-crusted pizzas, however, a pan is essential to support them while they cook. Round tray pans are made in diameters that range from 6 to 18 inches, while square ones are usually 12 or 14 inches and rectangular ones are commonly 12 by 16 inches. Nonstick coatings are preferable for easy removal. If you can find them, choose black-steel pans with rims of no more than ½ inch for easy removal of the pizza. Season and care for them as you would the deep-dish pan.

Cutting tray or board. There are thin metal trays made specifically for cutting and serving pizzas, although any similar tray will do. Alternatively, place the hot pizza on a wooden board for cutting, then transfer to a serving platter or individual plates.

CUTTING IMPLEMENTS

Select a *rolling wheel cutter* with a good sturdy handle and protective blade guards. My choice is a heavy-duty professional cutter with a metal handle and replaceable blade.

A good-quality *serrated bread knife* is perfect for cutting deep-dish and stuffed pizzas and can substitute for a rolling wheel cutter for slicing flat pizzas.

Look for a professional chef's *heavy-duty metal spatula* that's wide enough to lift whole pizzas onto plates.

Choose a wedge-shaped *serving spatula or pie server* for serving slices of large pizzas.

Basic Pizza Dough

1 tablespoon granulated sugar

1 cup warm (110° to 115° F.) water

1 envelope (¼ ounce) active dry yeast

3¼ cups bread, semolina, or
   unbleached all-purpose flour,
   or a combination

1 teaspoon salt

¼ cup olive oil, preferably extra-virgin

WHOLE-WHEAT VARIATION

1 tablespoon granulated sugar or
   honey

1¼ cups warm (110° to 115° F.) water

1 envelope (¼ ounce) active dry yeast

1¼ cups unbleached all-purpose flour

2 cups whole-wheat flour

1 teaspoon salt

¼ cup olive oil, preferably extra-
   virgin, or vegetable oil

This basic dough and its variations can be used for any type of pizza: traditional or contemporary; flat or deep-dish; topped, stuffed, or folded. The recipe can be doubled if you're entertaining a crowd or just want to prepare extra dough for freezing.

The Whole-Wheat Variation has a nutty, chewy texture that is compatible with hearty toppings. The Cornmeal Variation is reminiscent of the crusts used in many versions of Chicago-style deep-dish pizza; its crunch is appropriate with a wide variety of toppings. The New York Variation uses no sugar or oil, resulting in a crust that's drier throughout than the more flavorful Basic Dough, which has a crisp exterior and remains moist inside. Since pizza crusts and toppings are a matter of individual taste, try any crust with any topping; you can't go far wrong.

This very detailed recipe takes you through the steps necessary—mixing, kneading, shaping, and cooking—for creating all sizes and types of pizza. Read it through *several times* to become familiar with every element of pizza making before attempting any of the recipes.

In a small bowl, dissolve the sugar or honey (which "feeds" the yeast) in warm tap water that registers 110° to 115° F. For temperature accuracy, insert an instant-read thermometer in the water. Alternatively, learn to judge by touch; the water should be warm to your finger but not too hot—the temperature of a comfortable bath. Water that is too hot will kill the yeast, while water that is too cold will not activate it. (When making the New York Variation, omit the sugar and proceed as follows.) Sprinkle the yeast over the water and stir gently until it dissolves, about 1 minute. When yeast is mixed with the water at the proper temperature, a smooth, beige-colored mixture results. (If the yeast clumps together and the water stays clear, discard the mixture and start over). Let stand in a warm spot until a thin layer of foam covers the surface, about 5 minutes, indicating that the yeast is effective. (Discard mixture and start over with a fresh package of yeast if bubbles have not formed within 5 minutes.)

If making the whole-wheat dough, combine the 2 flours in a bowl and use as the flour in the directions that follow.

If making the cornmeal dough, combine the flour and cornmeal in a bowl and use the mixture as the flour in the directions that follow.

CORNMEAL VARIATION

1 tablespoon granulated sugar

1 cup warm (110° to 115° F.) water

1 envelope (¼ ounce) active dry yeast

2¼ cups unbleached all-purpose or semolina flour

1 cup yellow cornmeal or polenta (coarse cornmeal)

1 teaspoon salt

¼ cup olive oil, preferably extra-virgin, or vegetable oil

NEW YORK VARIATION

1 cup warm (110° to 115° F.) water

1 envelope (¼ ounce) active dry yeast

3¼ cups unbleached all-purpose flour

½ teaspoon salt

To mix and knead the dough by hand, combine 3 cups of the flour with the salt in a large mixing bowl. Make a well in the center of the flour and pour in the yeast mixture and the oil, if using. Using a wooden spoon, vigorously stir the flour into the well, beginning in the center and working toward the sides of the bowl, until the flour is incorporated and the soft dough just begins to hold together.

Turn the dough out onto a lightly floured surface. Dust your hands with flour and knead the dough gently in the following manner: press down on the dough with the heels of your hands and push it away from you, then partially fold it back over itself. Shift it a quarter turn and repeat the procedure. While kneading, very gradually add just enough of the remaining ¼ cup flour until the dough is no longer sticky or tacky; this should take about 5 minutes. As you work, use a metal dough scraper to pry up any bits of dough that stick to the work surface. Continue kneading until the dough is smooth, elastic, and shiny, 10 to 15 minutes longer. Knead the dough only until it feels smooth and springy; too much kneading overdevelops the gluten in the flour and results in a tough crust.

To mix and knead the dough in a heavy-duty food processor, add 3 cups of the flour and the salt to the beaker fitted with either a steel blade or a dough hook. Turn the machine on to combine the ingredients, about 5 seconds. Add the yeast mixture and oil, if using, and process continuously until the dough forms a single ball or several masses on top of the blade, about 30 seconds. Pinch off a piece of dough and feel it. If it is sticky, continue processing while gradually adding just enough of the remaining ¼ cup flour for the dough to lose its stickiness. If the dough is dry and crumbly, add warm water, a tablespoon at a time, until the dough is smooth. Turn the dough out onto a lightly floured surface and knead by hand as described above for about 2 minutes.

To mix and knead the dough in a heavy-duty standing electric mixer, combine 3 cups of the flour, the salt, yeast mixture, and oil, if using, in the large mixer bowl. Attach the flat beater, gradually turn on the machine to the medium speed, and beat until well mixed, about 1 minute. Replace the flat beater with the dough hook and knead at medium speed until the dough is smooth and elastic, about 5 minutes. Pinch off a piece of dough and feel it. If it is sticky, continue kneading while gradually adding just enough of the remaining ¼ cup flour for the dough to lose its stickiness. If the dough is dry and crumbly, add warm water, a tablespoon at a time, until the dough is smooth and elastic. It is not necessary to knead additionally by hand as with dough mixed in a food processor, unless you enjoy the process.

After mixing and kneading the dough by one of the above methods, shape the dough into a ball and place it in a well-oiled bowl, turning to coat completely on all sides with oil. (This oiling of the dough prevents a hard surface from forming that would inhibit rising.) Cover the bowl tightly with plastic wrap to prevent moisture loss, and set to rise in a draft-free warm place (75° F. to 85° F.—a hotter environment may kill the yeast) until doubled in bulk, about 45 minutes for quick-rising yeast or 1 to 1½ hours for regular yeast.

With your fist, punch down the dough as soon as it has doubled in bulk to prevent overrising. Shape it into a ball, pressing out all the air bubbles. If you are using bread flour or semolina flour, turn the dough in an oiled bowl to coat once more, cover the bowl tightly with plastic wrap and refrigerate it until puffy, from 35 minutes to 1 hour. Omit this step if using all-purpose flour.

If you cannot bake pizza within 2 hours after rising, punch the dough down again, turn it in an oiled bowl to coat once more, cover the bowl tightly with plastic wrap, and refrigerate. (The dough can be punched down a total of 4 times and kept refrigerated up to 36 hours before the yeast is exhausted and the dough unusable.) Let chilled dough come to room temperature before proceeding.

To make a 15- to 16-inch pizza, keep the dough in a single ball. To make two 12-inch round flat pizzas, two 10-inch calzone, two 9-inch deep-dish pizzas, or a double-crusted 10-inch round stuffed flat pizza, divide the dough into 2 equal-sized balls. To make a stuffed deep-dish pizza, divide the dough into 2 pieces, one twice as large as the other. To make individual 8-inch flat pizzas or calzone, divide the dough into 4 to 6 equal-sized portions. To make 3-inch appetizer-sized *pizzette* or calzone, divide the dough into 18 equal-sized portions.

If you wish to freeze dough for later use, wrap the pieces tightly in plastic wrap or seal in airtight plastic containers and freeze for up to 4 months. Before using, thaw in the refrigerator for 1 or 2 days or for a few hours at room temperature.

Shape the dough into circles by one of the following methods.

To shape by hand into an oiled deep-dish pizza pan, place a ball of dough in the pan and let it stand to soften for 10 minutes. Then flatten the dough with the heels of your hands and your fingertips to cover the bottom of the pan evenly. Pull the edge of the dough up the sides of the pan to form a 2-inch lip. Let the dough rise in the pan for about 20 minutes before filling and baking. For a thinner crust, fill and bake as quickly as possible. To form the top crust of a stuffed deep-dish pizza, see the following method for shaping a flat pizza.

To shape flat pizzas or calzone with a rolling pin, place a ball of dough on a lightly floured surface and dust the top of the dough lightly with flour. Using the heels of your hands, press the dough into a circle or other desired shape, then roll it out with a lightly floured rolling pin until it is about ¼ inch thick, keeping the edges a little thicker than the center. While rolling the dough, pick it up and turn it over several times to stretch it. Continue to keep the outer edges thicker than the rest of the pizza and add a little flour to the surface of the dough whenever needed to keep it from sticking. Rest one hand near the edge of the dough round and use the other hand to push the dough against it to form a slight rim around the dough, working your way completely around the perimeter of the dough. Lay the dough round on a cornmeal-dusted pizza peel or a lightly oiled pizza screen. Fill and bake as quickly as possible. To form the top crust of a stuffed deep-dish pizza (see page 24), use the rolling-pin method just described, rolling the dough circle to fit inside the pan; omit forming the rim.

To achieve a super-thin crust for a flat pizza or calzone by stretching, knead dough for about 1 minute. Lightly flour the work surface. Shape the dough into a flat disk about 1 inch thick and lightly flour both sides. Starting from the center of the dough, press it out quickly with the heels of your hands, working around the dough to create the desired shape, usually a circle, until the dough is about ½ inch thick. Dust with flour whenever needed to prevent sticking. Stop stretching before you reach the outer edge of the dough, which will form the rim of the pizza.

Rest one hand on the surface of the dough. Lift up a portion of the dough with the other hand and pull it gently away from the center, stretching it as thinly as possible. Continue moving around the dough, stretching it until it reaches the desired shape and size and is between ⅛ and ¼ inch thick. If a hole forms, pinch it closed. (Be very careful when shaping the cornmeal or whole-wheat variations by this method, as those doughs tear easily.) Now, rest one hand near the edge of the dough and use the other hand to push the dough against it to form a slight rim, working your way completely around the perimeter of the dough. Lay the stretched dough on a cornmeal-dusted pizza peel or a lightly oiled pizza screen. Fill and bake as quickly as possible.

Follow the individual recipes for topping or filling the dough.

For the crispiest crust, bake flat pizzas directly on a baking surface formed of unglazed quarry tiles or on a baking stone. In a gas oven, position the tiles or stone directly on the oven floor. In an electric stove, arrange the tiles or stone on the lowest rack of the oven. When using tiles, leave a 1-inch clearance between the tiles and the oven walls for air circulation. (See Equipment section for more information on the use of tiles and stones.) Preheat the oven at 500° F. for 1 hour before assembling the pizza. Before transferring the assembled pizza to the oven on a peel, give the peel a quick, short jerk to be sure the bottom of the crust has not stuck to it. Place the peel in the oven, holding the pizza over the stone or tiles, then quickly jerk the peel back 2 or 3 times, hopefully leaving the pizza centered on the cooking surface. (It takes practice, so don't be too discouraged if you lose a few pizzas.) Bake until the crust is golden or as directed in individual recipes, usually about 10 minutes. Slide the peel underneath the crust and remove the pizza from the oven. Use a metal spatula to lift a portion of the crust, if necessary, in order to slip the peel underneath.

You can bake as many pizzas at one time as the oven will accommodate; assemble one on the peel, transfer to the oven, then assemble the next one on the peel and transfer it to the oven. Continue the process, removing each pizza as soon as it is done. Do not cover a baked pizza with foil to keep it warm if you cannot serve it immediately; the crust will get soggy. If you wish to serve several pizzas at one time, it is best to bake them up to 1 hour ahead and reheat each one briefly, about 2 or 3 minutes, in a preheated 500° F. oven just before serving.

To bake on a pizza screen, brush the wire screen lightly with vegetable oil and top with the shaped dough. (A screen is the best way to bake pizzas with heavy toppings, as well as to cook several appetizer-sized *pizzette* or calzone at once.) Assemble the pizza as quickly as possible and give the screen a quick jerk to be sure the dough is not stuck to the wire. Place the screen directly on the hot tiles or pizza stone. If you choose not to use tiles or a stone, place the screen on the top rack of a preheated 500° F. oven to prevent the direct heat from burning the bottom crust. Bake until the crust is golden or as directed in individual recipes, usually about 10 minutes on tiles or a stone and about 15 minutes on an oven rack.

To bake calzone, place the dough on either a cornmeal-dusted peel or a lightly oiled screen. Fill and fold as quickly as possible, brush with oil as directed in the recipes, and transfer to a preheated 500° F. oven in the same way as flat pizzas. Calzone require slightly longer baking time, usually about 15 minutes, to achieve a puffed, golden brown crust and a piping-hot filling. To cook several calzone at a time, follow the suggestions on page 22.

Only deep-dish pizzas should be baked in a pan. Flat pizza crusts get too greasy and/or soggy when trapped in a pan. (See page 15.)

To bake in a deep-dish pan, press the dough into the pan as described on page 20, then prick the dough all over with the tines of a fork and place on the bottom rack of a preheated 475° to 500° F. oven for 4 minutes. Remove the crust from the oven, lightly brush with olive oil, and add the toppings. Return the pizza to the bottom rack of the oven for about 5 minutes, then move it to a rack in the middle of the oven and continue baking until the crust is golden, usually from 20 to 30 minutes.

To bake a stuffed deep-dish pizza, press the bottom crust into the pan as directed on page 20 and add the filling. Roll out the second piece of dough to fit just inside the pan (see page 21), center it over the filling, and press the crusts together to seal. Cut a 1-inch slit in the top crust to allow steam to escape during cooking, then gently press the top crust down over the filling. Start the pizza on the lowest rack of a preheated 475° to 500° F. oven for 10 minutes. Transfer the pan to the middle rack and bake until the crust is golden, usually 20 to 30 minutes. Some pizza bakers advocate covering the top crust with a tomato sauce before placing the pie in the oven; I prefer to add it during the final 10 minutes to avoid both overcooking the sauce and a soggy top crust.

To cut pizzas for serving, quickly jerk flat pizzas or calzone off the pizza peel or slide them off the wire screen onto a metal cutting tray or a wooden cutting board. Lift deep-dish pizzas from their pans onto the tray or board. With a cutting wheel or a serrated bread knife, quickly and firmly cut all the way across the pizza in several places to form wedges. Serve sliced large pizzas on the cutting tray or transfer to a platter. Serve sliced small pizzas or calzone on individual plates. With a serrated knife, cut large calzone crosswise into thick slices. Serve piping hot or at room temperature, depending on topping or filling.

Makes one 15- to 16-inch round flat pizza or deep-dish pizza; or two 12-inch round flat pizzas; or one double-crusted 10-inch round stuffed flat pizza; or two 9-inch round deep-dish pizzas; or one double-crusted 10-inch round stuffed deep-dish pizza; or two 10-inch folded calzone; or four to six 8-inch round individual pizzas; or 18 3-inch round appetizer-sized *pizzette* or calzone. Serves 4 to 6 as main course, 8 to 10 as a starter.

TRADITIONAL PIZZA

Here are pizzas from both sides of the Atlantic that have stood the test of time, be it centuries or decades.

Even with today's emphasis on gourmet pizza, it's hard to beat a properly made Neapolitan pie with its thin crust, garden-ripe tomatoes and basil, and fruity green olive oil. Several other standard offerings of Italian pizza bakers are also presented, with updated recipes for cooking them in home ovens. I've included two of the many versions of stuffed Italian pizza: the filled turnover called calzone and the *sfincione*, a thin double-crusted pie from Palermo.

Across the border, the French created their own form of pizza. Discover *pissaladière* and its topping of sweet caramelized onion accented by anchovies and oil-cured olives.

Pizza, New York style, is a variation of its Italian cousin. With its tomato sauce, mozzarella, and wide range of toppings, this East Coast classic is the major source of inspiration for pizzerias around the world.

According to a recent study by MRCA Information Services, Chicagoans consume more pizza per capita than folks in any other area of the country. The Windy City's deep-dish pizza is one of the great traditions born in the 1940s. A few pages farther on you'll learn how to make this justly famous adaptation of the Italian pie, as well as its stuffed double-crusted counterpart.

Fresh Tomato, Neapolitan Style (*Pizza alla Napolitana*)

Basic Pizza Dough (page 16)

Cornmeal, if using a pizza peel

About ½ cup olive oil, preferably extra-virgin

3 pounds vine-ripened Italian plum tomatoes, peeled and sliced, or peeled, seeded, chopped, and well drained, or 2 cans (28 ounces *each*) Italian plum tomatoes, well drained, seeded, and chopped

8 garlic cloves, thinly sliced or minced

½ cup whole fresh basil or oregano leaves, or 2 tablespoons chopped fresh basil or oregano, or 2 teaspoons dried oregano

Salt

Also known as *pizza alla marinara,* this Naples original depends for its success upon very flavorful tomatoes. Please don't attempt it with plastic-tasting supermarket varieties. Tradition calls for chopped seeded tomatoes and basil, but I prefer sliced peeled tomatoes and whole basil leaves.

Prepare the dough and preheat the oven as directed in the basic recipe beginning on page 16.

Roll out or stretch the pizza dough as directed for thin-crusted flat pizza on page 21. Place the dough on a pizza peel generously sprinkled with cornmeal or on a lightly oiled pizza screen. Brush dough all over with olive oil, then top with the tomatoes, leaving a ½-inch border around the edges. Sprinkle with the garlic, dried oregano, if using, and salt to taste. Drizzle evenly with olive oil.

Transfer the pizza to the preheated baking surface and bake until the crust is golden brown and puffy, about 10 minutes. Remove from the oven to a cutting tray or board and lightly brush the crust with olive oil. Top with basil or oregano. Slice and serve immediately.

Serves 4 to 6 as a main course, 8 to 10 as a starter.

Mozzarella and Tomato
(Pizza Margherita)

Created in honor of Italy's nineteenth-century Queen Margherita, who adored the peasant pie, this combination has become one of the world's most popular pizza presentations. Made with vine-ripened tomatoes, very fresh cheese, and the finest olive oil, it has no rivals.

Prepare the dough and preheat the oven as directed in the basic recipe beginning on page 16.

Roll out or stretch the pizza dough as directed for thin-crusted flat pizza in the basic recipe. Place the dough on a pizza peel generously sprinkled with cornmeal or on a lightly oiled pizza screen. Brush dough all over with olive oil, then evenly cover with the mozzarella cheese, leaving a ½-inch border around the edges. Cover the cheese with the tomatoes, then sprinkle with the oregano, salt to taste, and about half of the Parmesan cheese. Drizzle evenly with olive oil.

Transfer the pizza to the preheated baking surface and bake until the crust is golden brown and puffy, about 10 minutes. Remove from the oven to a cutting tray or board and lightly brush the crust with olive oil. Sprinkle with the remaining Parmesan cheese and the shredded basil, if available. Slice and serve immediately.

Serves 4 to 6 as a main course, 8 to 10 as a starter.

VARIATIONS: For all-white *pizza Margherita bianca,* omit the tomatoes. To make *pizza bianca alla romana,* omit the tomatoes and sprinkle 8 flat anchovy fillets, chopped, over the cheese.

Basic Pizza Dough (page 16)

Cornmeal, if using a pizza peel

About ½ cup olive oil, preferably extra-virgin

2½ cups (about 10 ounces) shredded fresh mozzarella cheese, preferably imported made in part from water buffalo's milk

4 cups peeled, seeded, chopped, and well-drained vine-ripened Italian plum tomatoes (about 2 pounds), or 1½ cans (28 ounces *each*) Italian plum tomatoes, well drained, seeded, and chopped

1 tablespoon minced fresh oregano, or 1 teaspoon dried oregano

Salt

½ cup (about 2 ounces) freshly grated Parmesan cheese, preferably Parmigiano Reggiano

½ cup shredded fresh basil (optional)

Four Seasons (*Quattro Stagioni*)

Basic Pizza Dough (page 16)

Cornmeal, if using a pizza peel

About ½ cup olive oil, preferably
 extra-virgin

¼ cup (about 1 ounce) freshly grated
 Parmesan cheese

6 ounces thinly sliced prosciutto

1 cup (about 4 ounces) shredded
 mozzarella cheese

1 cup peeled, seeded, chopped, and
 well-drained vine-ripened or
 canned Italian plum tomatoes

¾ cup chopped fresh or canned
 mussels or clams

1¼ cups thinly sliced fresh mushrooms,
 sautéed in 2 tablespoons olive oil

3 garlic cloves, minced or pressed

Salt

Minced fresh herbs such as parsley,
 oregano, basil, and thyme, and
 whole sprigs for garnish,
 preferably 4 different herbs

Divided by dough ropes into quarters containing ingredients that represent the subtle changing of the seasons in southern Italy, this is a far cry from what most Americans know as a "combination" pizza.

Prepare the dough and preheat the oven as directed in the basic recipe beginning on page 16.

Reserve one-fourth of the dough. Roll out or stretch the remaining pizza dough as directed for thin-crusted flat pizza in the basic recipe. Place the dough on a pizza peel generously sprinkled with cornmeal or on a lightly oiled pizza screen. Divide the reserved dough into 2 pieces and with palms of hands roll each piece into a ball and then into a cylinder about ⅓ inch in diameter; holding the cylinder at each end, twist in opposite directions to resemble a rope and place the 2 cylinders at right angles across the pizza crust to form even quarters. Brush the dough all over with olive oil. Leaving the dough ropes exposed and a ½-inch border around the outer rim, top one quarter of the dough with the Parmesan cheese, then the prosciutto. Fill another section with the mozzarella and ½ cup of the tomatoes. Fill the third section with the mussels or clams, and combine the mushrooms and remaining ½ cup tomatoes in the last section. Sprinkle the garlic over all the sections, add salt to taste, and drizzle evenly with olive oil.

Transfer the pizza to the preheated baking surface and bake until the crust is golden brown and puffy, about 10 minutes. Remove from the oven to a cutting tray or board and lightly brush the crust with olive oil. Sprinkle each section with one type minced herb and garnish with a sprig of the same herb. Slice and serve immediately.

Serves 4 as a main course, 8 as a starter.

Filled Turnovers (Calzone)

Basic Pizza Dough (page 16)

2 cups (about 8 ounces) shredded fresh mozzarella cheese

2 cups (about 1 pound) ricotta cheese

½ cup (about 2 ounces) freshly grated Parmesan cheese

Cornmeal, if using a pizza peel

About ½ cup olive oil, preferably extra-virgin

1 cup peeled, seeded, chopped, and well-drained vine-ripened or canned Italian plum tomatoes

5 ounces prosciutto or other flavorful ham, slivered

3 garlic cloves, minced or pressed (optional)

Salt

Freshly ground black pepper

In addition to classic pizza, Naples has also given the world the folded stuffed pizza. Almost any pizza topping can be used as a filling; here's a traditional favorite. Some people enjoy a simple tomato sauce poured over calzone when it comes out of the oven.

Prepare the dough and preheat the oven as directed in the basic recipe beginning on page 16.

In a large bowl, combine the mozzarella, ricotta, and ¼ cup of the Parmesan; reserve.

Roll out or stretch the pizza dough into circles as directed for calzone in the basic recipe. Working with 1 circle at a time, place the dough on a pizza peel generously sprinkled with cornmeal or on a lightly oiled pizza screen. Brush dough all over with olive oil, then cover half of dough circle with a generous portion of the cheeses, leaving a ½-inch border around the edges. Sprinkle with the tomatoes, prosciutto, garlic, and salt and pepper to taste. Fold the uncovered side over the filling and press the edges of the dough together to seal. Brush the dough with olive oil.

Transfer to the preheated baking surface and bake until the crust is golden brown and puffy, about 15 minutes. Remove from the oven to a plate, lightly brush with olive oil, sprinkle with Parmesan cheese, and serve immediately.

Serves 4 to 6 as a main course, 8 to 10 as a starter.

Stuffed, Palermo Style *(Sfincione)*

This Sicilian stuffed pie has roots in the meat-filled pies of the Middle East. It in turn is the likely inspiration for the popular Chicago-style double-crusted pizza.

Prepare the dough and preheat the oven as directed in the basic recipe beginning on page 16.

Heat about ¼ cup of the olive oil in a sauté pan or skillet over medium heat. Add the onion and cook until soft and golden, about 8 minutes. Transfer to a bowl to cool. Add the chopped or slivered meats and the cheeses to the cooled onion. Stir in the sun-dried tomatoes, garlic, parsley, oregano, and chili pepper to taste. Mix gently. Reserve.

Divide the pizza dough into 4 equal-sized pieces and roll out or stretch 1 piece into a circle or square as directed for thin-crusted flat pizza in the basic recipe. Place the dough circle or square on a pizza peel generously sprinkled with cornmeal or on a lightly oiled pizza screen. Brush the dough all over with olive oil, leaving a ½-inch border around the edges. Top with half the meat-and-cheese mixture and drizzle with olive oil.

Roll out or stretch a second piece of dough into a round or square large enough to cover the first. Place the dough over the stuffing and pinch the edges of the 2 sheets of dough together to seal tightly. Brush the top evenly with olive oil. Cut a 1-inch slit in the center for steam to escape during baking.

Transfer the pizza to the preheated baking surface and bake until the crust is golden brown and puffy, about 15 minutes. Remove from the oven to a cutting tray or board and lightly brush with olive oil. Repeat with remaining dough and ingredients. Let cool to room temperature before slicing and serving.

Serves 4 to 6 as a main course, 8 to 10 as a starter.

Basic Pizza Dough (page 16)

About ¾ cup olive oil, preferably extra-virgin

1 cup thinly sliced yellow onion

6 ounces thinly sliced prosciutto, chopped or slivered

6 ounces thinly sliced mild salami, chopped or slivered

6 ounces thinly sliced mortadella, chopped or slivered

½ cup (about 4 ounces) ricotta cheese

1 cup (about 6 ounces) shredded Italian Caciocavallo or Fontina cheese

About 10 sun-dried tomatoes in olive oil, well drained and chopped

6 garlic cloves, minced or pressed

¼ cup chopped fresh parsley

2 tablespoons minced fresh oregano, or 2 teaspoons dried oregano

Crushed dried red chili pepper

Cornmeal, if using a pizza peel

French Style *(Pissaladière)*

ONION SAUCE

¼ cup olive oil, preferably extra-virgin

6 cups thinly sliced red or yellow sweet onion (about 3 pounds)

6 garlic cloves, minced or pressed

3 tablespoons whole fresh thyme leaves, or 1 tablespoon dried thyme

1 bay leaf

Salt

Freshly ground black pepper

Basic Pizza Dough (page 16)

Cornmeal, if using a pizza peel

About ½ cup olive oil, preferably extra-virgin

12 flat anchovy fillets

1 cup oil-cured Niçoise or other ripe olives

1 tablespoon drained capers

1½ tablespoons pine nuts

In the south of France, the Italian savory pie idea took a new twist and a new name. The French call their version *pissaladière* after the olive-and-anchovy condiment *pissala*. Instead of round pies, the bakers of Provence often press the crust into rectangular baking sheets or tray pans.

To make the onion sauce, heat the olive oil in a sauté pan or skillet over medium heat. Add the onion, garlic, thyme, and bay leaf and cook, stirring occasionally, until most of the moisture has evaporated and the onion mixture is very soft, almost smooth, and caramelized, about 45 minutes. Discard the bay leaf and season the sauce to taste with salt and pepper. Remove from the heat and reserve. (The onion mixture may be stored in the refrigerator for several days or frozen for up to 4 months. Reheat before using.)

Prepare the dough and preheat the oven as directed in the basic recipe beginning on page 16.

Roll out the pizza dough as directed in the basic recipe. (Or press the dough into a 12-by-17-inch baking sheet.) Place the dough on a pizza peel generously sprinkled with cornmeal or on a lightly oiled pizza screen. Brush dough all over with olive oil, then cover with the reserved onion sauce, leaving a ½-inch border around the edges. Arrange the anchovies and olives over the onion base and sprinkle with the capers and pine nuts. Drizzle evenly with olive oil.

Transfer the *pissaladière* to the preheated baking surface and bake until the crust is golden brown and puffy, about 10 minutes. Remove from the oven to a cutting tray or board and lightly brush the crust with olive oil. Slice and serve immediately.

Serves 4 to 6 as a main course, 8 to 10 as a starter.

New York Style

TOMATO SAUCE

1 can (28 ounces) Italian plum
   tomatoes

2 tablespoons tomato paste

1 or 2 garlic cloves, minced or pressed

1 teaspoon dried basil or oregano

Salt

Freshly ground black pepper

Basic Pizza Dough, New York
   Variation (page 16)

Cornmeal, if using a pizza peel

About 1/2 cup olive oil, preferably
   extra-virgin

3 cups (about 12 ounces) shredded
   mozzarella cheese

3 garlic cloves, minced or pressed

Toppings, choose one or a
   combination: cooked and
   crumbled sweet Italian sausage,
   anchovy fillets, sautéed sliced
   fresh mushrooms, sliced
   pepperoni, sliced cooked Italian
   meatballs, sliced green or red
   sweet pepper, sliced red or yellow
   sweet onion, ripe olives, crushed
   dried red chili pepper (all optional)

1½ teaspoons dried oregano

⅓ cup (about 1½ ounces) freshly
   grated Parmesan cheese

Since the first pizzeria in New York—and in America—was opened by an immigrant *pizzaiolo* ("pizza baker") from Naples, it's no surprise that New York-style pizza is very similar to the Neapolitan pie. The principal departure from the original recipe was the use of tomato sauce in place of fresh tomatoes, full-flavored varieties of which were hard to come by on this side of the Atlantic. This pie became the standard of pizzerias coast to coast. The crust of a New York pizza is traditionally made without olive oil.

To make the tomato sauce, seed the tomatoes, if desired, and crush them with your hands or a fork in a heavy nonreactive saucepan over medium heat. Stir in the tomato paste, garlic, basil or oregano, and salt and pepper to taste. Bring the mixture just to a boil, then reduce the heat to low and simmer the sauce, stirring occasionally, until thick and flavorful, 30 minutes to 1 hour. Remove from the heat. (The sauce may be stored in the refrigerator for up to 1 week or frozen for up to 4 months.)

Prepare the dough and preheat the oven as directed in the basic recipe beginning on page 16.

Roll out or stretch the pizza dough as directed for thin-crusted flat pizza in the basic recipe. Place the dough on a pizza peel generously sprinkled with cornmeal or on a lightly oiled pizza screen. Brush dough all over with olive oil, then add the mozzarella cheese, leaving a ½-inch border around the edges. Top with the garlic and cover with the tomato sauce. Add one or more of the toppings, if desired, and sprinkle with the oregano and the Parmesan cheese. Drizzle evenly with olive oil.

Transfer the pizza to the preheated baking surface and bake until the crust is golden brown and puffy, about 10 minutes. Remove from the oven to a cutting tray or board and lightly brush the crust with olive oil. Slice and serve immediately.

Serves 4 to 6 as a main course, 8 to 10 as a starter.

Deep Dish, Chicago Style

Perhaps Chicago's major claim to culinary fame is the fabulous deep-dish pie with a chewy cornmeal crust that was developed by the founders of the renowned Pizzeria Uno in 1941. Like many Chicago pizzerias, you can choose to make the dough for deep-dish pizza without cornmeal; just use the Basic Pizza Dough. In addition to the standard topping options—sweet peppers, onion rings, anchovies, pepperoni—consider those featured in the New Pizza section.

Prepare the dough and preheat the oven to 475° F. as directed in the basic recipe beginning on page 16.

Crush the tomatoes in a bowl with your hands or a fork. Add the garlic, basil or oregano, and salt to taste. Reserve.

Press the dough into a 15-inch deep-dish pizza pan (or divide it in half and press each half into two 9-inch pans) as described in the basic recipe. Cover with plastic wrap and let the dough rise in a warm spot for about 20 minutes. Prick the bottom every ½ inch with the tines of a fork. Bake for 4 minutes, then remove from the oven and lightly brush the crust with olive oil.

Spread the mozzarella cheese completely over the bottom of the crust, then spoon on the tomatoes. Sprinkle with the Parmesan cheese and top with the sausage. Drizzle evenly with olive oil. Place on the bottom rack of the oven for 5 minutes, then move to a rack in the upper portion of the oven and bake until the crust is golden brown, the cheese is bubbly, and the sausage is cooked through, about 30 minutes. Remove from the pan to a cutting tray or board, lightly brush the crust with olive oil, slice, and serve immediately.

Serves 4 to 6 as a main course, 8 to 10 as a starter.

Basic Pizza Dough, Cornmeal Variation (page 16)

1 can (28 ounces) Italian plum tomatoes, seeded and drained

4 garlic cloves, minced or pressed

2 tablespoons minced fresh basil or oregano, or 2 teaspoons dried basil or oregano

Salt

About ½ cup olive oil, preferably extra-virgin

3 cups (about 12 ounces) shredded mozzarella cheese

½ cup (about 2 ounces) freshly grated Parmesan cheese

12 ounces lean Italian sausages, removed from casings and crumbled

Stuffed Deep Dish, Chicago Style

Basic Pizza Dough (page 16)

1 can (28 ounces) Italian plum tomatoes, seeded and drained

¼ cup chopped or shredded fresh basil, or 1½ teaspoons dried oregano

Salt

About 3 tablespoons olive oil, preferably extra-virgin

2 pounds fresh spinach, stems removed, thoroughly washed, dried, and finely chopped

5 garlic cloves, minced or pressed

Freshly ground black pepper or crushed dried red chili pepper

2½ cups (about 10 ounces) shredded mozzarella cheese

⅓ cup (about 1½ ounces) freshly grated Parmesan cheese

You can use the dough made with cornmeal if you like, although most Chicago pizzerias go with a basic dough for stuffed pizzas, which are thinner crusted than regular deep-dish pizzas. Substitute finely chopped, crisply cooked broccoli or mixed vegetables for the spinach; add crumbled lean Italian sausage or chopped Italian cold cuts along with or in place of the spinach.

Prepare the dough and preheat the oven to 475° F. as directed in the basic recipe beginning on page 16.

Crush the tomatoes in a bowl with your hands or a fork. Add the fresh basil or dried oregano and salt to taste; reserve.

Heat 1 tablespoon of the olive oil in a sauté pan or skillet over medium-high heat. Add the spinach and sauté just until it wilts. Stir in the garlic and season to taste with salt and black or red pepper. Transfer to a sieve to drain, pressing with the back of a wooden spoon to force out all moisture. Combine the drained spinach and the mozzarella in a bowl. Reserve.

Reserve one-third of the dough in the oiled bowl and cover with plastic wrap. Roll out the larger portion into a 14-inch circle and fit it into a 12-inch deep-dish pizza pan, pressing the dough onto the bottom and sides of the pan. Trim off the edge of the dough even with the rim of the pan. Fill the dough shell with the reserved spinach-and-mozzarella mixture.

Roll out the reserved dough portion into a 12-inch circle. Place on top of the filling and press the crusts together to seal. Cut a 1-inch slit in the center of the top crust to allow steam to escape during cooking, then gently press the top crust down over the filling. Brush the crust with olive oil.

Place the pie on the bottom rack of the oven for 10 minutes, then move to a rack in the upper portion of the oven and bake for 10 minutes. Remove from the oven and spoon the seasoned tomatoes over the top, then sprinkle with the Parmesan cheese. Return to the oven and bake until the bottom crust is golden brown, 10 to 15 minutes. (To check the bottom crust, use a spatula to lift a section.) Remove the pizza from the pan to a cutting tray or board, slice, and serve immediately.

Serves 4 to 6 as a main course, 8 to 10 as a starter.

NEW PIZZA

Thanks to the new breed of innovative American chefs, pizza, the country's number-one food, is experiencing a revolution. With a firm respect for the traditional Italian devotion to simple ingredients and absolute freshness, today's cooks are creating pizza that is a far cry from the bland sauce, canned mushroom, packaged Parmesan pie of red-checked-tablecloth pizzerias everywhere. While the Italians can take credit for having invented the savory pie and postwar Americans can be commended for popularizing it, it is the leaders of today's food renaissance who have elevated the pizza to gourmet status.

New pizza is exciting to cook, visually stimulating, tastes fantastic, and is guaranteed to make most people rethink their notions about this ubiquitous dish.

In this section I've included my own interpretations of a few ideas gleaned from eating at my favorite purveyors of pizza, California cuisine style—Spago in Los Angeles, California Pizza Kitchen in Beverly Hills, Vicolo in San Francisco, and the Café at Chez Panisse in Berkeley. You'll also find several pizzas that are totally of my own invention.

Not all of the recipes may appeal to you; try those that suit your taste. Armed with the basic dough recipe and the detailed directions for forming, assembling, and baking pizza found at the beginning of the book, you can begin creating your own original pizzas.

Chèvre, Sun-Dried Tomatoes, and Roasted Garlic

The classic California cuisine trio—goat's milk cheese, sun-dried tomatoes, and roasted garlic—creates a sensation on a crisp crust moistened with flavorful olive oil.

To roast the garlic, preheat the oven to 300° F.

Place the garlic cloves in a small baking dish and toss with 3 tablespoons of the olive oil. Cover the dish and bake until the cloves are tender but not browned, about 30 minutes. Remove from the oven, cool, and chop; reserve.

Prepare the dough and preheat the oven as directed in the basic recipe beginning on page 16.

Shape the pizza dough as directed in the basic recipe. Brush dough all over with olive oil, then top with the mozzarella and chèvre, leaving a ½-inch border around the edges. Sprinkle with the reserved garlic, the tomatoes, parsley, and salt and pepper to taste. Drizzle evenly with olive oil or, if you like, the oil in which the tomatoes were packed.

Transfer the pie to the preheated baking surface and bake as directed in the basic recipe. Remove from the oven to a cutting tray or board and lightly brush the crust with olive oil or oil in which the tomatoes were packed. Sprinkle with flowers and Parmesan cheese. Slice and serve immediately.

Serves 4 to 6 as a main course, 8 to 10 as a starter.

10 to 12 garlic cloves

About ½ cup plus 3 tablespoons olive oil, preferably extra virgin

Basic Pizza Dough (page 16)

Cornmeal, if using a pizza peel

2 cups (about 8 ounces) shredded mozzarella cheese

2 cups (about 8 ounces) crumbled California chèvre or other goat's milk cheese

About 12 sun-dried tomatoes in olive oil, well drained and slivered

¼ cup minced fresh parsley

Salt

Freshly ground black pepper

Pesticide-free nasturtium, onion, and/or garlic flowers, rinsed, dried, and shredded (optional)

¼ cup (about 1 ounce) freshly grated Parmesan cheese

Primavera

Basic Pizza Dough (page 16)

1 pound fresh young asparagus, tough stems discarded and tender stalks cut into 2-inch pieces on the diagonal

1 pound fresh broccoli, florets only

12 ounces fresh tiny green or yellow summer squash, sliced

1 cup shelled fresh green peas (about 8 ounces)

Cornmeal, if using a pizza peel

About ½ cup olive oil, preferably extra-virgin

2 cups (about 8 ounces) shredded mozzarella cheese

2 cups (about 6 ounces) shredded white Cheddar cheese

1 cup sliced cherry tomatoes, preferably yellow-fleshed variety

6 green onions, chopped (optional)

Salt

Freshly ground black or white pepper

¼ cup (about 1 ounce) freshly grated Parmesan cheese

3 tablespoons minced fresh tarragon

Spring's arrival is celebrated in this presentation of tender garden vegetables. Who says a pizza has to be a traditional circle or rectangle? To make a triangle, press the ball of dough into the desired shape with your hands and then flatten and stretch it as you would a round pie.

Prepare the dough and preheat the oven as directed in the basic recipe beginning on page 16.

Separately steam or blanch the asparagus, broccoli, squash, and peas until crisp tender; immerse immediately in ice water to halt cooking and retain bright color. Drain well and reserve.

Shape the pizza dough as directed in the basic recipe. Brush dough all over with olive oil, then top with the shredded cheeses, leaving a ½-inch border around the edges. Arrange the blanched or steamed vegetables and tomatoes on top of the cheese. Sprinkle with the green onions and season to taste with salt and pepper. Drizzle evenly with olive oil.

Transfer the pie to the preheated baking surface and bake as directed in the basic recipe. Remove from the oven to a cutting tray or board and lightly brush the crust with olive oil. Sprinkle with the Parmesan cheese and tarragon, slice, and serve immediately.

Serves 4 to 6 as a main course, 8 to 10 as a starter.

Pesto

Even though today pesto sauce is being made out of parsley, spinach, cilantro, or almost anything green, I still prefer the classic recipe using fresh basil. Pesto can be made up to several days ahead and stored in the refrigerator with a thin layer of olive oil over the top to prevent darkening. Since cooking destroys the delicate flavor of basil, I always top the melted cheese with the sauce the moment the pie comes out of the oven. If you wish to make pesto calzone, mix the sauce with the cheese, fill and fold the dough, and bake like other calzone. In either case, a crunchy cornmeal crust is especially good.

To make the pesto, combine the basil leaves, garlic, and pine nuts in a blender or food processor and purée to desired smoothness. Add the cheeses and blend briefly. Pour in the olive oil and mix well. Reserve.

Prepare the dough and preheat the oven as directed in the basic recipe beginning on page 16.

Shape the dough as directed in the basic recipe. Prick the dough all over with the tines of a fork and brush with olive oil, then top with the mozzarella and Fontina cheeses, leaving a ½-inch border around the edges. Drizzle evenly with olive oil.

Transfer the pie to the preheated baking surface and bake as directed in the basic recipe. Remove from the oven to a cutting tray or board and lightly brush the crust with olive oil. Spoon on the pesto, sprinkle with the Parmesan cheese, and garnish with the basil and pine nuts. Slice and serve immediately.

Serves 4 to 6 as a main course, 8 to 10 as a starter.

VARIATION: If you enjoy the tanginess of goat's cheese, substitute crumbled chèvre for part of the cheese in the pesto, then use more of it to cover the pizza along with, or in place of, the Fontina.

PESTO

2 cups firmly packed whole fresh basil leaves, washed and dried

3 garlic cloves

½ cup pine nuts

½ cup (about 2 ounces) freshly grated Parmesan cheese, preferably Parmigiano Reggiano

¼ cup (about 1 ounce) freshly grated Pecorino Romano cheese

½ cup olive oil, preferably extra-virgin

Basic Pizza Dough or Cornmeal Variation (page 16)

Cornmeal, if using a pizza peel

About ½ cup olive oil, preferably extra-virgin

2 cups (about 8 ounces) shredded mozzarella cheese

1 cup (about 5 ounces) shredded Italian Fontina cheese

¼ cup (about 1 ounce) freshly grated Parmesan cheese, preferably Parmigiano Reggiano

Tiny whole fresh green or purple basil leaves or shredded fresh basil for garnish

Pine nuts for garnish

Eggplant and Chèvre

Mediterranean flavors make this a perfect lunch for a sun-drenched day. Sautéed ground lamb or beef seasoned with tomato sauce and oregano may be layered between the cheese and the eggplant.

Prepare the dough and preheat the oven as directed in the basic recipe beginning on page 16.

Trim the blossom ends of the eggplant so that the pieces measure in length one-half of the diameter of the pizza you intend to make. Sprinkle both sides of the eggplant slices generously with salt and place on a rack to drain for about 30 minutes. (Salting the eggplant reduces moisture and cuts down on the amount of oil that will be absorbed during cooking.) Rinse the eggplant, drain, and press between paper towels to dry.

Heat a large heavy skillet over medium heat. Brush the eggplant slices on both sides with olive oil and arrange as many as will fit in a single layer in the skillet. Cook on the first side until lightly browned, about 2 minutes; turn and cook on the second side until lightly browned. Remove to a plate and reserve. Repeat with remaining eggplant slices.

Shape the pizza dough as directed in the basic recipe. Brush dough all over with olive oil, then top with the bûcheron, leaving a ½-inch border around the edges. Sprinkle with the garlic and the *herbes de Provence.* Arrange the eggplant slices in a pinwheel pattern, slightly overlapping the slices. Top with the fiddleheads, if using. Season to taste with salt and pepper and drizzle evenly with olive oil.

Transfer the pie to the preheated baking surface and bake as directed in the basic recipe. Remove from the oven to a cutting tray or board and lightly brush the crust with olive oil. Sprinkle with the Parmesan cheese and garnish with the rosemary. Slice and serve immediately.

Serves 4 to 6 as a main course, 8 to 10 as a starter.

Basic Pizza Dough (page 16)

10 slender Japanese eggplants, or 6 small globe eggplants (about 2½ pounds), blossom ends discarded, sliced lengthwise into ¼-inch-thick slices

About ⅔ cup salt

About 1 cup olive oil, preferably extra-virgin

Cornmeal, if using a pizza peel

3 cups (about 12 ounces) crumbled bûcheron or other goat's milk cheese

4 to 6 garlic cloves, minced or pressed

1 tablespoon dried *herbes de Provence,* or to taste

Fresh fiddleheads (newly emerged fern fronds; optional)

Salt

Freshly ground black pepper

⅓ cup (about 1½ ounces) freshly grated Parmesan cheese, preferably Parmigiano Reggiano

Fresh rosemary for garnish

Avocado, Tomato, and Basil

The flavors of a California summer melt together in this rendition. Try cherry tomatoes if you can't locate other tasty varieties.

Prepare the dough and preheat the oven as directed in the basic recipe beginning on page 16.

Shape the pizza dough as directed in the basic recipe. Brush dough all over with olive oil, then top with 1½ cups of the Parmesan cheese, leaving a ½-inch border around the edges. Arrange the tomatoes, onion rings, and avocado slices on top of the cheese and season to taste with salt and pepper. Drizzle evenly with olive oil.

Transfer the pie to the preheated baking surface and bake as directed in the basic recipe. Remove from the oven to a cutting tray or board and lightly brush the crust with olive oil. Sprinkle with the remaining ½ cup Parmesan and the basil. Slice and serve immediately.

Serves 4 to 6 as a main course, 8 to 10 as a starter.

Basic Pizza Dough or Whole-Wheat Variation (page 16)

Cornmeal, if using a pizza peel

About ½ cup olive oil, preferably extra-virgin

2 cups (about 8 ounces) freshly grated Parmesan cheese, preferably Parmigiano Reggiano

1½ pounds vine-ripened tomatoes, peeled and sliced

1 red sweet onion, very thinly sliced and separated into rings

2 ripe avocadoes, halved, pitted, scooped from the peel, and thinly sliced

Salt

Freshly ground black pepper

¾ cup shredded or chopped fresh basil

Black Olive and Red Pepper

Basic Pizza Dough (page 16)

3 large red sweet peppers

Cornmeal, if using a pizza peel

About ½ cup olive oil, preferably extra-virgin

2½ cups (about 10 ounces) shredded mozzarella cheese

5 or 6 flat anchovy fillets, minced (optional)

4 garlic cloves, minced or pressed

2½ cups drained pitted ripe olives, preferably oil-cured, finely chopped

Salt

Freshly ground black pepper

Red and black toppings create a dramatic and tasty pizza.

Prepare the dough and preheat the oven as directed in the basic recipe beginning on page 16.

Hold the peppers over an open flame or slip under a broiler and turn frequently until completely charred on all sides. Place the peppers in a loosely closed paper bag until cool, about 15 minutes. Remove the peppers from the bag and rub off blackened skin with fingertips. Cut peppers in half lengthwise, remove and discard seeds and veins, and finely chop. Reserve.

Shape the pizza dough as directed in the basic recipe. Brush dough all over with olive oil, then top with the cheese, leaving a ½-inch border around the edges. Sprinkle with the anchovies and garlic, then arrange the reserved red peppers and the olives to form alternating stripes or in a checkerboard design. Season to taste with salt and pepper and drizzle evenly with olive oil.

Transfer the pie to the preheated baking surface and bake as directed in the basic recipe. Remove from the oven to a cutting tray or board and lightly brush the crust with olive oil. Slice and serve immediately.

Serves 4 to 6 as a main course, 8 to 10 as a starter.

Wild Mushrooms

Earthy wild mushrooms blend beautifully with the flavor and aroma of smoked cheese. The nutty texture of a whole-wheat crust is perfect for this pizza. If you can find 4 varieties of wild mushroom, roll one-fourth of the dough into ropes and divide the pizza into sections as described on page 32. Cook each mushroom variety separately, then fill each section with a different mushroom for comparing tastes.

Prepare the dough and preheat the oven as directed in the basic recipe beginning on page 16.

Slice or chop the fresh mushrooms, combine them with the sherry or port, and let stand for about 30 minutes. If using dried mushrooms, leave them whole and combine them with the sherry or port; let stand until very soft, about 1 hour. Drain off soaking liquid in either case. Rinse the dried mushrooms very thoroughly to remove all grit, drain, squeeze out moisture, and slice or chop.

Heat the butter in a sauté pan or skillet over medium heat, add the mushrooms, and sauté until tender, about 5 minutes. Season to taste with salt and pepper. Remove from the heat and reserve.

Shape the pizza dough as directed in the basic recipe. Brush dough all over with walnut or olive oil, then top with the cheese, leaving a ½-inch border around the edges. Distribute the mushrooms over the cheese and drizzle evenly with walnut or olive oil.

Transfer the pie to the preheated baking surface and bake as directed in the basic recipe. Remove from the oven and lightly brush the crust with walnut or olive oil. Sprinkle with the thyme and pink pepperberries, slice, and serve immediately.

Serves 4 to 6 as a main course, 8 to 10 as a starter.

Basic Pizza Dough, Whole-Wheat Variation (page 16)

1½ pounds fresh wild mushrooms, such as *chanterelles,* morels, *porcini,* or *shiitakes,* or ¾ pound dried wild mushrooms

1½ cups dry sherry or port

¼ pound (1 stick) unsalted butter

Salt

Freshly ground black pepper

Cornmeal, if using a pizza peel

About ½ cup walnut oil or olive oil, preferably extra-virgin

3 cups (about 12 ounces) shredded smoked Provolone or Gouda cheese

2 tablespoons whole fresh thyme leaves

Pink pepperberries (dried fruit of *Schinus molle* tree) for garnish

Three Caviars

Basic Pizza Dough (page 16)

Cornmeal, if using a pizza peel

About ½ cup olive oil, preferably extra-virgin

2 cups (about 1 pound) sour cream

3 ounces black caviar

6 ounces red caviar

12 ounces golden caviar

Whole fresh chives for garnish

Pesticide-free nasturtium flowers for garnish (optional)

Make these elegant little pizzas, topped with the best caviar your budget allows, as appetizers or first courses. If you wish, pass chopped hard-cooked egg, minced chives, and lemon wedges for squeezing at the table.

Prepare the dough and preheat the oven as directed in the basic recipe beginning on page 16.

Shape the pizza dough as directed in the basic recipe. Prick dough all over with the tines of a fork, then brush with olive oil.

Transfer the pie to the preheated baking surface and bake as directed in the basic recipe. Remove from the oven to a cutting tray or board and spoon on sour cream, leaving a ½-inch border around the edges. Arrange the 3 caviars on top, creating a bull's-eye design or other pattern. Garnish with the chives and nasturtiums, if using. Serve immediately.

Serves 8 to 10 as a starter.

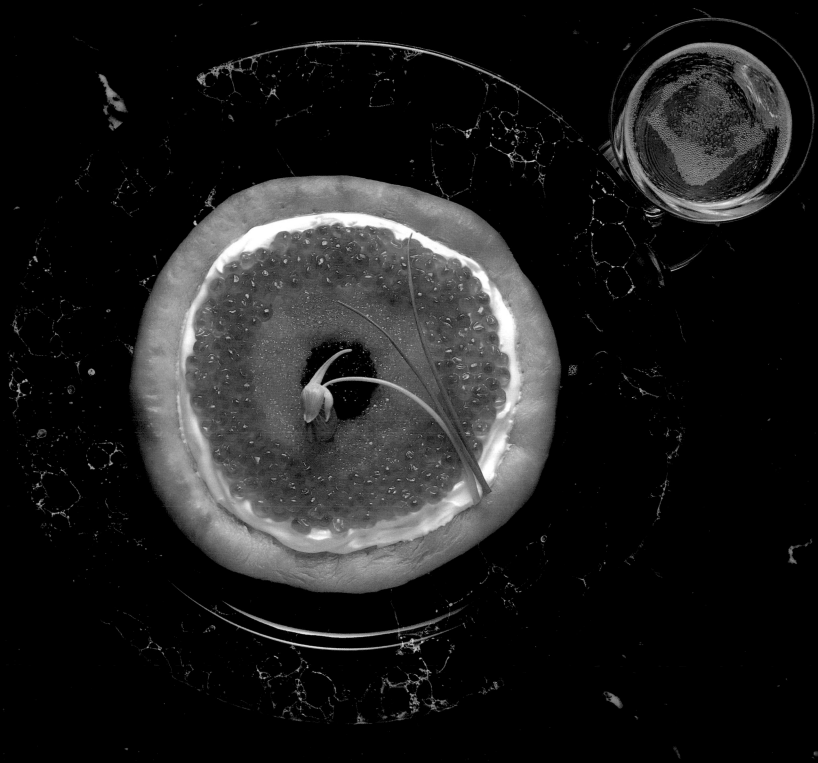

Smoked Salmon and Brie

Basic Pizza Dough (page 16)

Cornmeal, if using a pizza peel

About 1/2 cup olive oil, preferably extra-virgin

1 pound Brie cheese, rind discarded, cut into small pieces

12 ounces smoked salmon, cut into small pieces

1 small red sweet onion, very thinly sliced, separated into rings, and rings quartered

Fresh dill sprigs for garnish

Serve this opulent concoction for brunch, or in small portions to begin a dinner.

Prepare the dough and preheat the oven as directed in the basic recipe beginning on page 16.

Shape the pizza dough as directed in the basic recipe. Prick dough all over with the tines of a fork, then brush with olive oil.

Transfer the pie to the preheated baking surface and bake until the crust just begins to brown, about 6 minutes. Remove from the oven and cover with the cheese, leaving a ½-inch border around the edges. Arrange the salmon and onion on top and drizzle evenly with olive oil. Return to the oven and bake until the crust is golden brown and puffy, the cheese begins to melt, and the salmon is heated through, about 4 minutes. Remove from the oven to a cutting tray or board and lightly brush the crust with olive oil. Garnish with the dill. Slice and serve immediately.

Serves 4 to 6 as a main course, 8 to 10 as a starter.

Mixed Seafood

Basic Pizza Dough or Cornmeal
   Variation (page 16)

Cornmeal, if using a pizza peel

About ½ cup olive oil, preferably
   extra-virgin

2 cups (about 8 ounces) grated
   Gruyère cheese

8 ounces scallops, cut into bite-sized
   pieces if large

8 ounces small to medium-sized
   shrimp, peeled and deveined

8 ounces squid, cleaned, tentacles
   reserved, and bodies sliced into
   ¼-inch-wide rings, or cooked crab
   meat, picked over

5 or 6 garlic cloves, or to taste,
   minced or pressed

1 tablespoon freshly grated lemon
   zest, or to taste

¾ cup (about 3 ounces) freshly
   grated Parmesan cheese

Salt

Freshly ground black or white pepper

Whole fresh chives or minced fresh
   parsley

Scallops, squid, and shrimp accented with garlic and lemon are bedded on melted cheese in this seafood extravaganza. There's no need to precook the seafood; the brief intense heat is ample.

Prepare the dough and preheat the oven as directed in the basic recipe beginning on page 16.

Shape the pizza dough as directed in the basic recipe. Prick the dough all over with the tines of a fork, brush with olive oil, and top with the Gruyère cheese, leaving a ½-inch border around the edges. Drizzle with olive oil.

Transfer the pie to the preheated baking surface and bake about 6 minutes. Remove from the oven and top the cheese with the seafood. Sprinkle with the garlic, lemon zest, and ½ cup of the Parmesan cheese. Season to taste with salt and pepper. Return pizza to the oven and bake until the seafood is cooked and the crust is golden brown and puffy, about 4 minutes. Remove from the oven to a cutting tray or board and lightly brush the crust with olive oil. Sprinkle with the remaining ¼ cup Parmesan cheese and garnish with chives or parsley. Slice and serve immediately.

Serves 4 to 6 as a main course, 8 to 10 as a starter.

VARIATION: Top the cheese with a favorite fresh tomato sauce, or use the New York-style tomato sauce on page 40.

Kung Pao Shrimp

Basic Pizza Dough (page 16)

2 pounds medium-sized shrimp

2 tablespoons cornstarch

½ cup rice wine vinegar

¼ cup soy sauce

¼ cup granulated sugar

¼ cup peanut oil

1 large green sweet pepper, seeded, deveined, and cut into small chunks

2 medium-sized carrots, quartered lengthwise and thinly sliced

½ cup thinly sliced canned miniature corn on the cob (optional)

6 green onions, thinly sliced

3 tablespoons chopped fresh ginger root

2 tablespoons minced or pressed garlic

7 to 10 small dried red chili peppers

¾ cup roasted peanuts

About ½ cup Asian-style hot sesame or hot chili oil

Cornmeal, if using a pizza peel

Miniature corn on the cob for garnish (optional)

Whole fresh cilantro (coriander) leaves for garnish

East truly meets West in this cheeseless pizza topped with spicy stir-fried shrimp. You may, of course, add a layer of cheese if you wish. The amount of hot oil you brush on the dough probably seems like a lot, but it takes that much to flavor the crust.

Prepare the dough and preheat the oven as directed in the basic recipe beginning on page 16.

Peel, devein, rinse, and dry the shrimp. Reserve.

In a small bowl, combine the cornstarch, vinegar, soy sauce, and sugar. Reserve.

Heat 2 tablespoons of the peanut oil in a wok or deep-sided skillet over high heat until hot. Add the shrimp and stir-fry until they turn bright pink, about 2 minutes. Remove the shrimp to a bowl. Heat the remaining 2 tablespoons peanut oil in the wok, add the green pepper, carrots, corn, green onions, ginger, garlic, chili peppers, and peanuts. Stir-fry until the vegetables are coated with the oil, about 1 minute. Add the reserved cornstarch mixture and bring to a boil. Add the reserved shrimp and stir until they are well coated with the sauce. Remove from the heat, season to taste with hot sesame or chili oil, and reserve.

Shape the pizza dough as directed in the basic recipe. Brush dough all over with hot oil and prick all over with a fork.

Transfer the pie to the preheated baking surface and bake about 5 minutes. Remove from the oven and top with the reserved shrimp mixture, leaving a ½-inch border around the edges. Return to the oven and cook until the crust is golden brown and puffy, about 5 minutes. Remove from the oven to a cutting tray or board and lightly brush the crust with hot oil. Garnish with the miniature corn, if using, and cilantro. Slice and serve immediately.

Serves 4 to 6 as a main course, 8 to 10 as a starter.

Clams, Mussels, and Vermont Cheddar

This scrumptious New England feast was suggested by my friend Mary Val McCoy, who divides her time between Vermont and California. In the photograph, I've divided the pizza equally between clams and mussels.

Prepare the dough and preheat the oven as directed in the basic recipe beginning on page 16.

Shape the pizza dough as directed in the basic recipe. Brush dough all over with olive oil, then top with the Cheddar cheese, leaving a ½-inch border around the edges. Top the cheese with the clams and/or mussels, then sprinkle with the garlic and salt and white pepper to taste. Drizzle evenly with olive oil.

Transfer the pie to the preheated baking surface and bake as directed in the basic recipe. Remove from the oven to a cutting tray or board and lightly brush the edges of the crust with olive oil. Sprinkle the top with the Parmesan cheese, parsley, and chili pepper to taste. Slice and serve immediately.

Serves 4 to 6 as a main course, 8 to 10 as a starter.

Basic Pizza Crust, Cornmeal Variation (page 16)

Cornmeal, if using a pizza peel

About ½ cup olive oil, preferably extra-virgin

4 cups (about 12 ounces) shredded Vermont or other high-quality Cheddar cheese, preferably natural white (not orange dyed)

5 cups freshly shucked and drained small clams and/or mussels, or 4 cans (10 ounces *each*) small whole clams, drained

6 to 8 garlic cloves, minced or pressed

Salt

Freshly ground white pepper

½ cup (about 2 ounces) freshly grated Parmesan cheese

Fresh parsley leaflets, preferably flat-leaf Italian type for garnish

Crushed dried red chili pepper

Barbecued Chicken

It was love at first bite when I tasted a creation that combined two of my favorite foods—cheese pizza and barbecued chicken—at the new wave California Pizza Kitchen in Beverly Hills. Here is my version of the ethereal concoction. Use your favorite made-from-scratch tomato-based barbecue sauce or any good-quality commercial sauce. The chicken can be prepared on the grill or in the oven as long as a day before you bake the pizza.

Combine the chicken and 1 cup of the barbecue sauce in a bowl and marinate in the refrigerator for at least 4 hours (or as long as overnight). Return the chicken to room temperature before cooking.

Place the chicken breasts and their marinade in an ovenproof dish, cover with foil, and cook in a preheated 325° F. oven until tender and just past the pink stage inside, about 30 minutes. Let the chicken cool, then cut the meat into bite-sized pieces. (Alternatively, grill the chicken over a moderate charcoal fire.)

Prepare the dough and preheat the oven as directed in the basic recipe beginning on page 16.

Shape the pizza dough as directed in the basic recipe. Brush dough all over with olive oil, then top with a layer of each of the cheeses, leaving a ½-inch border around the edges. Using the remaining 2 cups of barbecue sauce, spoon a layer of sauce over the cheeses. Arrange the chicken and onion rings on top and drizzle evenly with olive oil.

Transfer the pie to the preheated baking surface and bake as directed in the basic recipe. Remove from the oven to a cutting tray or board and lightly brush the crust with olive oil. Sprinkle with the cilantro or oregano, slice, and serve immediately.

Serves 4 to 6 as a main course, 8 to 10 as a starter.

5 boned and skinned chicken breast halves

3 cups tomato-based barbecue sauce

Basic Pizza Dough (page 16)

Cornmeal, if using a pizza peel

About ½ cup olive oil, preferably extra-virgin

1½ cups (about 8 ounces) shredded Italian Fontina cheese

1½ cups (about 6 ounces) shredded smoked Gouda cheese

1 red sweet onion, very thinly sliced and separated into rings

¼ cup chopped fresh cilantro (coriander) or fresh oregano

Garlic-Glazed Chicken

Basic Pizza Dough or Whole-Wheat
    Variation (page 16)

¼ cup sesame seeds

2 heads garlic, broken into cloves,
    peeled, and coarsely chopped

2 teaspoons crushed dried red
    chili pepper

½ cup soy sauce

5 tablespoons honey

1½ cups rice wine vinegar

About ¾ cup vegetable oil

5 boned and skinned chicken breast
    halves, cut into bite-sized pieces

Cornmeal, if using a pizza peel

2 cups (about 8 ounces) grated
    Gruyère cheese

1 cup (about 4 ounces) shredded
    mozzarella cheese

¼ cup chopped green onions

Even garlic lovers might be alarmed by the huge quantity of the aromatic bulb, but it turns sweet and succulent during the cooking.

Prepare the dough and preheat the oven as directed in the basic recipe beginning on page 16.

Put the sesame seeds in a small skillet over medium heat. Toast the seeds, stirring or shaking the pan, until golden, about 4 minutes. Empty onto a plate to cool. Reserve.

Combine the garlic, crushed red pepper, soy sauce, honey, and vinegar in a bowl. Reserve.

Heat ¼ cup of the vegetable oil in a sauté pan or large skillet over medium-high heat and sauté chicken until opaque on all sides, about 3 minutes. Remove with a slotted spoon and reserve. Pour the garlic mixture into the skillet and cook over medium-high-heat, stirring frequently, until the sauce is reduced to the consistency of syrup, about 15 minutes. Return the chicken to the pan and cook, stirring constantly, until the pieces are lightly glazed, about 2 minutes. Remove from the heat and reserve.

Shape the dough as directed in the basic recipe. Brush dough all over with vegetable oil, then top with a layer of each of the cheeses and the glazed chicken, leaving a ½-inch border around the edges. Sprinkle with the green onions. Drizzle evenly with vegetable oil.

Transfer the pie to the preheated baking surface and bake as directed in the basic recipe. Remove from the oven to a cutting tray or board and lightly brush the crust with vegetable oil. Sprinkle with the toasted sesame seeds, slice, and serve immediately.

Serves 4 to 6 as a main course, 8 to 10 as a starter.

Thai Chicken

MARINADE

¼ cup *each* finely chopped onion, celery, and carrot

3 garlic cloves, minced or pressed

1 tablespoon minced shallot

2 teaspoons minced fresh ginger root

1 teaspoon freshly grated lime zest

1 teaspoon crushed dried red pepper

3 large sprigs fresh cilantro (coriander)

1 tablespoon brown sugar

⅓ cup soy sauce

⅓ cup freshly squeezed lime juice

2 tablespoons crunchy peanut butter

2 tablespoons peanut oil

5 boned chicken breast halves

Basic Pizza Dough (page 16)

Cornmeal, if using a pizza peel

About ½ cup peanut or hot chili oil

1½ cups (about 8 ounces) shredded Italian Fontina cheese

1½ cups (about 6 ounces) shredded mozzarella cheese

4 green onions, thinly sliced

1 medium-sized carrot, peeled and cut into fine julienne

1½ cups bean sprouts

½ cup coarsely chopped dry-roasted peanuts

⅓ cup chopped fresh cilantro

Chicken breasts are smothered in fragrant Southeast Asian seasonings and baked before topping this truly exotic pizza.

To make the marinade, combine the onion, celery, carrot, garlic, shallot, ginger root, lime zest, chili pepper, cilantro, brown sugar, soy sauce, lime juice, peanut butter, and peanut oil in a bowl. Mix thoroughly, then add the chicken breasts, cover, and refrigerate at least 8 hours or for up to 2 days. Return the chicken to room temperature before baking.

Place the chicken and the marinade in an ovenproof dish, cover with foil, and bake in a 325° F. oven until the chicken is tender, about 30 minutes. Let the chicken cool, then discard the skin and shred the meat or chop into very small pieces. (The chicken may be cooked up to 1 day in advance of preparing the pizza.)

Prepare the dough and preheat the oven as directed in the basic recipe beginning on page 16.

Shape the pizza dough as directed in the basic recipe. Brush dough all over with peanut or hot chili oil, then top with a layer of each of the cheeses, leaving a ½-inch border around the edges. Strew the cooked chicken over the cheeses and sprinkle with the green onions, carrot, bean sprouts, and peanuts. Drizzle evenly with peanut or hot chili oil.

Transfer the pie to the preheated baking surface and bake as directed in the basic recipe. Remove from the oven to a cutting tray or board and lightly brush the crust with peanut or hot chili oil. Sprinkle with the cilantro, slice, and serve immediately.

Serves 4 to 6 as a main course, 8 to 10 as a starter.

Smoked Pheasant

Many types of smoked fowl can be purchased in gourmet stores and some supermarkets. Substitute smoked chicken or duck if pheasant is not available. When you can't find small tender leeks, use green onions.

Prepare the dough and preheat the oven as directed in the basic recipe beginning on page 16.

Toss the leeks with 2 tablespoons of the walnut or olive oil and season to taste with salt and pepper. Reserve.

Shape the pizza dough as directed in the basic recipe. Brush dough all over with walnut or olive oil, then top with the cheese, leaving a ½-inch border around the edges. Distribute the garlic and all but ¼ cup of the reserved leeks over the cheese. Season to taste with salt and pepper. Drizzle evenly with walnut or olive oil.

Transfer the pie to the preheated baking surface and bake for 5 minutes. Remove from the oven, arrange the pheasant over the top, and continue cooking until the pheasant is warmed through and the crust is golden brown and puffy, about 5 minutes. Remove from the oven to a cutting tray or board and lightly brush the crust with walnut or olive oil. Sprinkle with the remaining leeks, slice, and serve immediately.

Serves 4 to 6 as a main course, 8 to 10 as a starter.

VARIATION: Substitute slices of grilled rabbit for the smoked fowl.

Basic Pizza Dough (page 16)

5 small leeks, white and tender green portions only, cut into 1½-inch-long very fine julienne

About 1/2 cup walnut oil or olive oil, preferably extra-virgin

Salt

Freshly ground black pepper

Cornmeal, if using a pizza peel

3 cups (about 15 ounces) shredded Italian Fontina cheese

5 garlic cloves, minced or pressed

One 2-1/2- to 3-pound smoked pheasant, boned and meat cut into bite-sized pieces or shredded

BLT

A pizza inspired by two sandwich favorites—bacon, lettuce, and tomato and grilled cheese.

Prepare the dough and preheat the oven as directed in the basic recipe beginning on page 16.

Heat ¼ cup of the olive oil in a sauté pan or large skillet over medium heat. Add the chopped greens, cover, and cook just until the greens are wilted, about 45 seconds. Stir in the garlic and cook, uncovered, until the greens are just tender, about 2 minutes. Cool and drain well in a sieve, pressing out excess moisture with the back of a wooden spoon.

Shape the pizza dough as directed in the basic recipe. Brush dough all over with olive oil, then cover with the cheese, leaving a ½-inch border around the edges. Top with the sautéed greens, bacon, and tomatoes. Season to taste with salt and pepper. Drizzle evenly with olive oil.

Transfer the pie to the preheated baking surface and bake as directed in the basic recipe. Remove from the oven to a cutting tray or board and lightly brush the crust with olive oil. Slice and serve immediately.

Serves 4 to 6 as a main course, 8 to 10 as a starter.

Basic Pizza Dough (page 16)

¾ cup olive oil, preferably extra-virgin

1½ pounds fresh greens such as romaine lettuce, beet tops, chicory, dandelion, escarole, or spinach, tough stems removed, washed, dried, and coarsely chopped

4 garlic cloves, minced or pressed

Cornmeal, if using a pizza peel

3 cups (about 12 ounces) grated Gruyère or shredded smoked mozzarella cheese

1 pound bacon, fried crisp and crumbled

2 cups peeled, seeded, chopped, and well-drained vine-ripened tomatoes

Salt

Freshly ground black pepper

Hawaiian Pineapple and Canadian Bacon

I had to be convinced that this popular Pacific Coast recipe was worthy of inclusion. Following extensive taste-testings, I have arrived at the opinion that it's actually quite good, but definitely not for pizza traditionalists.

Prepare the dough and preheat the oven as directed in the basic recipe beginning on page 16.

Mix the cheeses in a bowl and set aside.

Shape the pizza dough as directed in the basic recipe. Brush dough all over with vegetable oil, then top with the cheeses, leaving a ½-inch border around the edges. Top the cheeses with the Canadian bacon or ham, pineapple chunks, onions, and salt and pepper to taste. Drizzle evenly with vegetable oil.

Transfer the pie to the preheated baking surface and bake as directed in the basic recipe. Remove from the oven to a cutting tray or board and lightly brush the crust with vegetable oil. Slice and serve immediately.

Serves 4 to 6 as a main course, 8 to 10 as a starter.

Basic Pizza Dough (page 16)

1½ cups (about 6 ounces) shredded mozzarella cheese

1½ cups (about 6 ounces) grated Gruyère cheese

Cornmeal, if using a pizza peel

About ½ cup vegetable oil

1 pound Canadian bacon or baked ham, cut into small pieces

3 cups chopped fresh pineapple, or 3 cans (8 ounces *each*) chunk pineapple packed in juice, well drained

6 green onions, chopped

Salt

Freshly ground black pepper

Mu Shu Pork

Traditionally eaten rolled up in a mandarin pancake, here stir-fried pork and eggs is accented with sweet *hoisin* sauce and green onions atop a cheeseless pizza.

Prepare the dough and preheat the oven as directed in the basic recipe beginning on page 16.

In a bowl, combine the soy sauce, rice wine or sherry, cornstarch, and sugar and mix well. Add the slivered pork and toss well. Let stand about 5 minutes.

Heat a wok or deep-sided skillet over high heat until hot. Add about 2 tablespoons peanut oil, reduce the heat to medium, and add the eggs. Cook, stirring constantly, just until the eggs are set. Scrape them out into a bowl and reserve.

Return the wok or skillet to the heat and add 2 more tablespoons peanut oil. Add the marinated pork mixture and stir-fry just until the meat is no longer pink, about 5 minutes. Add the lily buds and cloud ears or mushrooms and stir-fry until heated through, about 1 minute. Remove from the heat and stir in the cooked eggs. Season to taste with sesame oil, if using, and salt to taste. Reserve.

Shape the pizza dough as directed in the basic recipe. Brush dough all over with sesame or peanut oil, then spoon on a layer of the *hoisin* sauce, leaving a ½-inch border around the edges. Top the *hoisin* with the stir-fried pork-and-egg mixture and drizzle evenly with sesame or peanut oil.

Transfer the pie to the preheated baking surface and bake as directed in the basic recipe. Remove from the oven to a cutting tray or board and lightly brush the crust with sesame or peanut oil. Sprinkle with the green onions, slice, and serve immediately.

Serves 4 to 6 as a main course, 8 to 10 as a starter.

Basic Pizza Dough (page 16)

2 tablespoons soy sauce

1½ tablespoons Chinese rice wine or dry sherry

1½ teaspoons cornstarch

2 teaspoons granulated sugar

¾ pound boned pork shoulder, thinly sliced and then cut into slivers 2 inches long by 1 inch wide

¼ cup peanut oil for stir-frying

6 eggs, lightly beaten

¾ cup dried tiger lily buds (about 45 buds), soaked in warm water for 30 minutes, then hard tips broken off and discarded and buds sliced in half crosswise

8 dried cloud ears or black Chinese mushrooms, soaked in warm water for 30 minutes, then drained and chopped (discard hard stems and other portions)

About ½ cup Asian-style sesame oil or peanut oil

Salt

Cornmeal, if using a pizza peel

About 1 cup *hoisin* sauce

6 green onions, cut into 1-inch-long pieces and then slivered

Chorizo, Cheese, and Chilies

Basic Pizza Dough (page 16)

1 pound good-quality chorizo or other spicy pork sausages

About ⅔ cup vegetable oil

½ cup finely chopped yellow onion

1 teaspoon minced or pressed garlic

3 tablespoons good-quality chili powder, or to taste, if not using spicy chorizo

1 teaspoon ground cumin, or to taste

Cornmeal, if using a pizza peel

2 cups (about 6 ounces) shredded Monterey Jack cheese

2 cups (about 6 ounces) shredded white Cheddar cheese

2 cups well-drained cooked dried or canned chili or pinto beans

1 cup chopped fresh or canned mild or hot chili peppers

1 cup finely chopped red sweet onion

Crushed dried red chili pepper

¼ cup (about 1 ounce) freshly grated Parmesan cheese

⅓ cup chopped fresh cilantro (coriander)

Homemade or commercial red or green salsa

South-of-the-border seasonings are surprisingly compatible with the Italian pie. For a milder flavor, use ground beef or chopped cooked chicken in place of the spicy sausage. For the photograph, I've made appetizer-sized calzone using cornmeal dough and wrapped them in corn husks so that they are reminiscent of tamales.

Prepare the dough and preheat the oven as directed in the basic recipe beginning on page 16.

Remove the chorizo from casings, crumble, and place in a skillet over medium heat and cook until done. Remove from the skillet and drain on paper towels; discard the grease in the skillet. Pour 2 tablespoons vegetable oil into the skillet over medium heat, add the yellow onion, and cook until soft, about 5 minutes. Add the drained chorizo, the garlic, chili powder, if using, and cumin and cook to combine flavors, about 2 minutes. Remove from the heat and reserve.

Shape the pizza dough as directed in the basic recipe. Brush dough all over with vegetable oil, then top with a layer of each of the cheeses, leaving a ½-inch border around the edges. Cover the cheeses with the reserved chorizo mixture, then arrange the beans, chopped chili peppers, and red onion over the top. Season to taste with crushed red pepper. Drizzle evenly with vegetable oil.

Transfer the pie to the preheated baking surface and bake as directed in the basic recipe. Remove from the oven to a cutting tray or board and lightly brush the crust with vegetable oil. Sprinkle with the Parmesan cheese, cilantro, and salsa. Slice and serve immediately.

Serves 4 to 6 as a main course, 8 to 10 as a starter.

Chili con Carne

Very popular in Texas, chili-topped pizza can be made mild or fiery to suit your taste buds. Use your own favorite chili recipe, or try this one, my sister Martha's claim to culinary fame, albeit with a few of my own modifications. Prepare it up to three days in advance of cooking the pizza.

I prefer this pizza made in a deep-dish pan. Do not attempt to use this recipe to make large flat pizzas. The chili is too heavy for the crust and it will collapse without a pan for support.

To make the chili, heat the oil in a dutch oven or other heavy pot over medium heat. Add the onion and cook until soft, about 5 minutes. Add the ground beef and garlic and cook until the meat is just past the pink stage. Add the chili powder, cumin, flour, and salt, black pepper, and cayenne pepper to taste; mix well. Stir in the tomato sauce, cover, reduce the heat, and simmer until the flavors are well blended, about 1 hour. Add a little water during the cooking if the mixture dries out. You want the chili to be just a bit on the dry side to keep the pizza crust from getting soggy during baking.

Prepare the dough and preheat the oven as directed in the basic recipe beginning on page 16.

Shape the pizza dough as directed in the basic recipe. Brush dough all over with vegetable oil, then cover with about half of each cheese, leaving a ½-inch border around the edges. Top with the chili, then sprinkle with the onion and cover with the remaining cheese.

Transfer the pie to the preheated baking surface and bake as directed in the basic recipe. Remove from the oven to a cutting tray or board and lightly brush the crust with vegetable oil. Garnish with cilantro, slice, and serve immediately.

Serves 4 to 6 as a main course, 8 to 10 as a starter.

CHILI CON CARNE

3 tablespoons vegetable oil

2 cups finely chopped yellow onion

3 pounds ground lean beef

4 garlic cloves, minced or pressed, or to taste

¾ cup good-quality chili powder, or to taste

1 tablespoon ground cumin, or to taste

½ cup unbleached all-purpose flour

Salt

Freshly ground black pepper

Ground cayenne pepper

3 cans (7 ounces *each*) tomato sauce

Basic Pizza Dough, Cornmeal Variation (page 16)

Cornmeal, if using a pizza peel

About ¼ cup vegetable oil

2 cups (about 6 ounces) shredded Monterey Jack cheese

2 cups (about 6 ounces) shredded yellow Cheddar cheese

½ cup minced red sweet onion

Fresh cilantro (coriander) leaves for garnish

Caramelized Onion and Sausage

1 cup olive oil, preferably
  extra-virgin

6 cups thinly sliced yellow sweet onion
  (about 3 pounds)

Salt

Freshly ground black pepper

4 or 5 garlic cloves, minced or pressed

¾ pound hot Italian sausage, cooked
  and sliced into ½-inch-thick pieces

½ cup dry white wine

3 tablespoons chopped fresh parsley

Basic Pizza Dough (page 16)

Cornmeal, if using a pizza peel

2 cups (about 10 ounces) shredded
  Italian Fontina cheese

2 cups (about 8 ounces) shredded
  mozzarella cheese

½ cup (about 2 ounces) freshly grated
  Parmesan cheese

Red sweet pepper, julienned,
  for garnish

Fresh parsley sprigs, preferably
  flat-leaf Italian type, for garnish

Onion slowly cooked until sweetly caramelized is counterpointed with zesty sausage. The topping can be made up to two days in advance.

Heat ½ cup of the olive oil in a large heavy skillet over medium heat. Add the onion, stir to coat with the oil, reduce the heat to medium-low, cover, and cook, stirring occasionally, until the onions are soft and have just begun to color, about 30 minutes. Remove the cover, sprinkle with salt and pepper to taste, increase the heat to medium, and cook uncovered, stirring frequently, until the onion is deep golden and caramelized, about 25 minutes.

Add the garlic and sausage slices to the onions. Place over high heat, stir in the wine, and cook, stirring constantly, until the wine is reduced but the mixture is still moist, about 3 minutes. Stir in the chopped parsley.

Prepare the dough and preheat the oven as directed in the basic recipe beginning on page 16.

Shape the pizza dough as directed in the basic recipe. Brush dough all over with olive oil, then top with the Fontina and mozzarella cheeses, ¼ cup of the Parmesan cheese, and the onion and sausage mixture, leaving a ½-inch border around the edges. Drizzle evenly with olive oil.

Transfer the pie to the preheated baking surface and bake as directed in the basic recipe. Remove from the oven to a cutting tray or board and lightly brush the crust with olive oil. Sprinkle with the remaining ¼ cup Parmesan cheese and garnish with sweet pepper and parsley sprigs. Slice and serve immediately.

Serves 4 to 6 as a main course, 8 to 10 as a starter.

VARIATIONS: Substitute cooked pork tenderloin for the sausages. Sauté apple slices and/or cooked pitted prunes along with the onion. For a vegetarian dish, omit the pork.

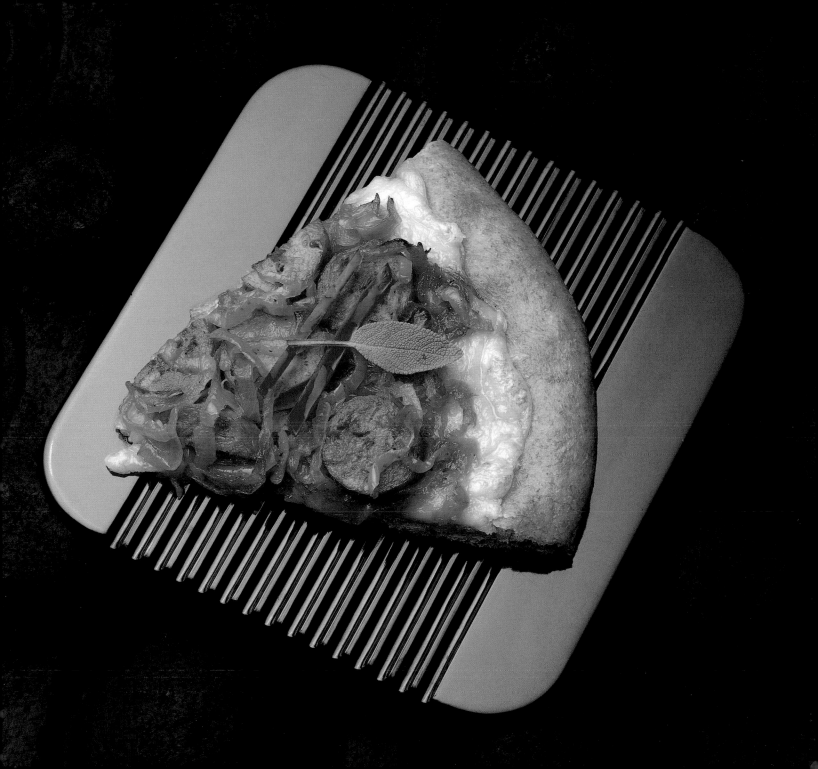

Fruit and Cheese

Pizza purists may frown at the idea, but this combination results in a tasty brunch dish or unusual dessert.

Prepare the dough and preheat the oven as directed in the basic recipe beginning on page 16, adding the granulated sugar to the flour. Use vegetable oil in place of the olive oil.

Melt 6 tablespoons butter in a sauté pan or skillet over medium heat. Add the apples and sauté them until they are tender but still hold their shape, about 10 minutes; cover the pan for the last few minutes of cooking. When the apples are almost done, stir in the brown sugar and the cinnamon to taste. Reserve.

Shape the pizza dough as directed in the basic recipe. Prick dough all over with the tines of a fork and brush it with melted butter.

Transfer the pie to the preheated baking surface and bake until the crust just begins to brown, about 6 minutes. Remove from the oven and cover with the cheese, leaving a ½-inch border around the edges. Arrange the apples in an overlapping pinwheel pattern over the cheese. Return to the oven and bake until the crust is golden brown and puffy and the cheese is warmed through and beginning to melt, about 4 minutes. Remove from the oven to a cutting tray or board and lightly brush the crust with melted butter. Garnish with mint leaves. Slice and serve immediately. Accompany with small scoops of ice cream, whipped cream, or crème fraîche, if desired.

Serves 6 to 8 as a brunch course, 8 to 10 as a dessert.

VARIATION: To make the strawberry and chocolate confection shown, partially bake the crust as described, then top with chocolate cream cheese or the triple crème. Return to the oven to finish cooking and to soften the cheese. Remove the pizza from the oven and drizzle it with a favorite warm chocolate sauce. Top with fresh hulled strawberries, garnish, and serve as for pizza.

Basic Pizza Dough (page 16), made with vegetable oil and ¼ cup granulated sugar

6 tablespoons unsalted butter

5 or 6 flavorful apples such as Gravenstein or McIntosh, peeled (if desired), cored, and thinly sliced

½ cup firmly packed light brown sugar

Ground cinnamon

Cornmeal, if using a pizza peel

About ⅓ cup unsalted butter, melted

1 pound St.-André or other triple crème cheese, rind discarded, cut into 1-inch cubes

Whole fresh mint leaves for garnish

Good-quality vanilla ice cream, unsweetened whipped cream, or crème fraîche (optional)

Index

Recipe Index

Acknowledgments

To Nion McEvoy for convincing Chronicle Books of the validity of this project. To the other staff members of Chronicle Books for their continued assistance in a host of invaluable ways.

To my sister Martha McNair, my brother-in-law John Richardson, and my nephew Devereux McNair for their hospitality and eager willingness to taste-test Los Angeles pizzas.

To Mary McCoy for helping to organize me during the writing phase.

To Carrie Crotty of Pizzas in Paradise, St. Johns, Antigua, for helpful suggestions.

To Lew Gallo of Yosh for my new look.

To Bill Nightingale and Kitchens Italia, San Francisco, for use of the Schiffini Cucine Design kitchen on page 7 and the back cover flap.

To Glenn Carroll for finding the huge hunk of lava.

To Till of Clervi Marble Company, San Francisco, for the loan of backgrounds.

To Gail High for keeping the kitchen in order and for sacrificing her yeast-free diet to sample the pizzas baked daily in the studio ovens.

To Sheryl Scott for so quickly learning how to make the numerous *caffè latte* essential to the photography.

To Patricia Brabant, an inspired photographer who has added immeasurable creativity to my work and pleasure to my life.

To Addie Prey, Buster Booroo, Joshua J. Chew, and Michael T. Wigglebutt for all their dedicated taste-testing.

And to Lin Cotton, the best partner and friend anyone could ever wish for.